Jungle Rescue

Books by Christina G. Miller and Louise A. Berry

COASTAL RESCUE: Preserving Our Seashores
JUNGLE RESCUE: Saving the New World Tropical Rain Forests

JUNGLE RESCUE

Saving the New World Tropical Rain Forests

CHRISTINA G. MILLER
and
LOUISE A. BERRY

Illustrated with photographs and a map

ATHENEUM 1991 NEW YORK

Collier Macmillan Canada
Toronto
Maxwell Macmillan International Publishing Group
New York Oxford Singapore Sydney

Atheneum
Macmillan Publishing Company
866 Third Avenue
New York, NY 10022

Collier Macmillan Canada, Inc.
1200 Eglinton Avenue East
Suite 200
Don Mills, Ontario M3C 3N1

First edition
Printed in the United States of America
1 2 3 4 5 6 7 8 9 10

Book Production by Daniel Adlerman
Printed on not less than fifty percent recycled paper

Library of Congress Cataloging-in-Publication Data
Miller, Christina G.
Jungle rescue: saving the New World tropical rain forests / by Christina G. Miller and Louise A. Berry.
p. cm.
Includes bibliographical references.
Summary: In order to avoid a global ecological crisis, the alarming destruction of the tropical rain forests of Central and South America must be reversed.
ISBN 0-689-31487-6
1. Rain forest ecology—South America—Juvenile literature. 2. Forest conservation—South America—Juvenile literature. 3. Rain forest ecology—Central America—Juvenile literature. 4. Forest conservation—Central America—Juvenile literature. [1. Rain forest ecology—South America. 2. Forest conservation—South America. 3. Rain forest ecology—Central America. 4. Forest conservation—Central America. 5. Ecology.] I. Berry, Louise A. II. Title.
QH111.M58 1991
574.5'2642'098—dc20 90-1150 CIP AC

JUNGLE RESCUE by Christina G. Miller and Louise A. Berry
Photo Credits: Frederick J. Dodd - International Zoological Expeditions:
Cover, 2, 10, 13, 15, 22, 23, 24, 26, 33, 36, 38, 45, 46, 47, 48, 91, 94, 97, 104
Andrew L. Young: 42, 48
Mark J. Plotkin: 52
Lou Ann Dietz: 57
Thomas Stone, Research Associate, Woods Hole Research Center, Woods Hole, MA 02543: 63, 64, 86
World Bank Photo Library: 66, 69, 71, 102
John A. West: 73
U.S. Fish and Wildlife Service: 99

Dedicated to the survival of Panthera onca

ACKNOWLEDGMENTS

We would like to thank the following people for being valuable resources to us as we researched material for this book:

Dr. Rob Bierregaard
Principal Investigator
Biological Dynamics of Forest Fragments Project
Smithsonian Institution

Ms. Lou Ann Dietz
Brazil Program Officer
World Wildlife Fund

Dr. Russell A. Mittermeier
President
Conservation International

Charles Roover
Attorney-at-Law

Dr. Karen B. Strier
Assistant Professor
Department of Anthropology
University of Wisconsin—Madison

We are grateful for permission to use the resources of the Cabot Science Library of Harvard University and for the valuable assistance of Martha J. Cohen, librarian at the Massachusetts Audubon Society's Hathaway Environmental Resource Library.

CONTENTS

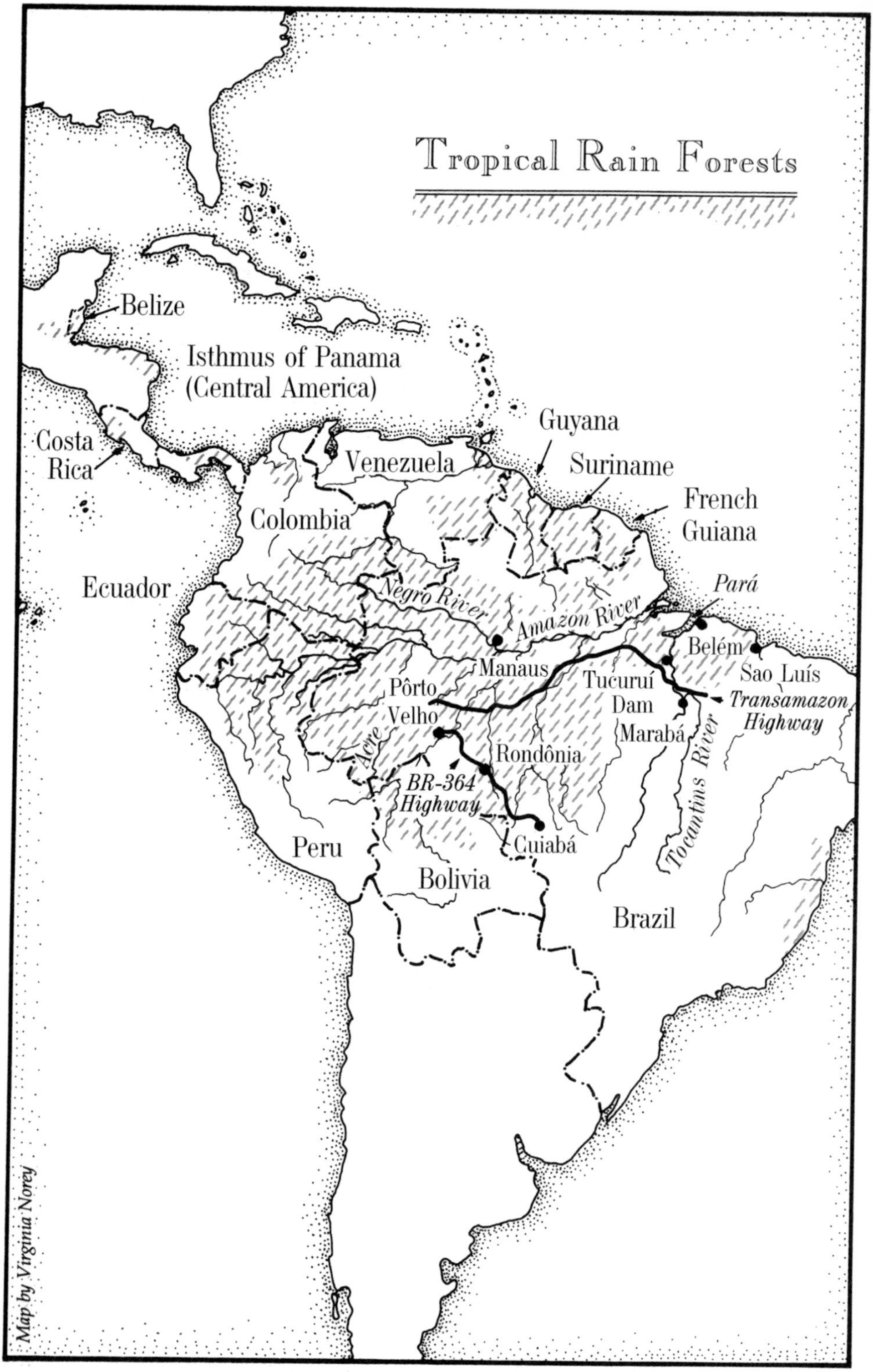
Tropical Rain Forests
Belize
Isthmus of Panama
(Central America)
Costa
Rica
Venezuela
Guyana
Suriname
French
Guiana
Colombia
Ecuador
Negro River
Amazon River
Pará
Belém
Sao Luís
Manaus
Tucuruí
Dam
Marabá
Transamazon
Highway
Pôrto
Velho
Acre
Rondônia
Tocantins River
BR-364
Highway
Cuiabá
Peru
Bolivia
Brazil
Map by Virginia Norey

1
Understanding the Tropical Rain Forest

Wherever you may live in the United States you've almost certainly walked through a forest. Most forests in North America are *temperate forests.* However, few Americans have ever visited the jungles of a tropical rain forest. Your impression of what a jungle is like might be based on stories such as Rudyard Kipling's *Jungle Books,* movies such as *Tarzan, The Emerald Forest,* and *Gorillas in the Mist,* and even on television cartoons. Some of the plants and animals that live in the rain forest are so unusual that it is difficult to believe they are not imaginary but actually exist. The rain forests in Central and South America are home to the largest rodent in the world, the peaceful capybara; to strange creatures including the anteater and the vampire bat; to colorful parrots, macaws, and other exotic birds; to giant snakes such as the anaconda; and to large beautiful orchids, and vines that are as thick as a person's body and grow hundreds of feet long.

When anteaters find an insect nest, they rip it apart with their sharp claws and lick up the fleeing insects with their sticky tongues.

However, now the rain forest plants and animals are in trouble. Around the world every day people cut down or burn thousands and thousands of acres of rain forest to obtain its wood and minerals or so that the land can be used for pasture and crops. This rapid destruction is thought to be one of the most serious problems of our time. The importance of the rain forests to humankind extends far beyond the boundaries of the nations in which they are found. By understanding the *ecology* of the rain forest and the reasons for its destruction, you can become part of the worldwide jungle rescue presently underway.

To help you find where the tropical rain forests are located, you will want to use a globe. First put your finger on the equator and then move it upward toward the Arctic Circle until you see the parallel of latitude called the Tropic of Cancer. This is the top of the tropical "belt." Next move your finger downward about the same distance from the equator to the parallel of latitude called the Tropic of Capricorn. This is the bottom of the tropical belt, or the *Tropical Zone.* The continental United States is located in the *Temperate Zone.* This is the part of the earth lying between the Tropic of Cancer and the Arctic Circle in the Northern *Hemisphere* and between the Tropic of Capricorn and the Antarctic Circle in the Southern Hemisphere.

Once you have found the tropics on the globe, you can locate the rain forests. The rain forests in Africa and Asia are commonly called the Old World tropical rain forests. In Africa they are primarily around the Zaire River, which forms the Congo Basin in central Africa, along the Gulf of Guinea in West Africa, and on the coast of the island of Madagascar in the Indian Ocean.

Long ago the earth wore a broad tropical green belt of rain forests around its middle that covered nearly 12 percent of its entire land surface. Asian rain forests once covered large parts of southeast Asia including major land areas in India, Bangladesh, and Indochina. However, people have destroyed so many of the rain forests that they are now found mainly in western India, Burma, Thailand, Sri Lanka, Malaysia, the Philippines, Borneo, Sumatra, and the Celebes. In addition to

Africa, Asia, and some islands in the Pacific and Caribbean, rain forests are located in Central and South America.

This book is about lowland tropical moist forests that are located in the Western Hemisphere. They are commonly referred to as New World tropical rain forests. They grow in the tropics at low altitudes, as opposed to mountaintops, and are damp. New World tropical rain forests are found in parts of Central and South America and on some Caribbean islands as well as in parts of Mexico, Costa Rica, Belize, and Panama. However, the largest remaining rain forest in the world is in the Amazon Basin in South America. Called "Amazonia," this area is about two-thirds the size of the continental United States. It stretches eastward from the foothills of the Andes Mountains in Bolivia, Peru, Ecuador, and Colombia across Brazil to the Atlantic Ocean.

The Amazon River, the second-longest river in the world, flows through Amazonia carrying billions of gallons of water per hour to the Atlantic Ocean at its eastern end. Some of the rivers flowing into the Amazon are larger than the Mississippi River. During the rainy season parts of the Amazon become swollen with so much water that it surges over the river's banks and floods the forest. In these areas, the river rises to the height of a two-story house. Animals that live in the lower parts of the forest survive by clinging to trees and plants above the water level, and fish swim through the submerged tree branches. People construct their houses on stilts and farmers build log rafts for their cattle and horses.

In the tropics seasonal changes depend mainly on the differences in the amount of rainfall. The seasons are not clearly marked by temperature differences as they are in the Temperate Zone. Near the equator it is warm and humid year round. Your newspaper probably has a weather section with climate data. Using this information you can keep a record of temperatures in the Temperate and Tropical zones. (If the "mean temperature" is reported this has been figured by adding the day's high and low temperatures and dividing by two.)

Make a chart by putting the date of the newspaper in the left-hand margin of a piece of paper. Write the name of a place near where you live as well as the names of tropical cities such as Rio de Janeiro, Brazil; Caracas, Venezuela; and Lima, Peru for which weather data is often reported, at the top of the page. About every two weeks record the date and degrees Fahrenheit (F) in columns under the various locations. How do the seasonal temperatures in the Temperate Zone where you live compare with those of places in the Tropical Zone?

The four distinct seasons in the Temperate Zone are caused by the turning of the earth on its axis. An axis is a straight line around which something spins or rotates. Look again at your globe and find the earth's axis, the imaginary line between the North and South poles. The pointer over the North and South poles shows either end of the earth's axis. Notice that the globe is mounted on its stand in such a way as to show how the earth spins on its tilting axis when it rotates around the sun.

The earth spins on its axis once every twenty-four hours. When North America is facing the sun it is daylight there and night on the other side of the world. It takes the earth one year to revolve around the sun. During this year-long journey different parts of the earth receive different amounts of sunlight because the earth is tilted on its axis. To demonstrate this ask a friend to be the sun and walk around your friend in a circle while you hold the globe tilted on its axis. When the top of the earth's axis points toward the sun it is summer in the Northern Hemisphere. The Northern Hemisphere receives more sunlight and temperatures are much warmer than when the north axis leans away from the sun and it is winter in the Temperate Zone.

At noontime on a winter day your shadow is long. This is because the Northern Hemisphere is tipped away from the sun and sunlight does not come from overhead but falls at a low angle. More of the sun's energy is absorbed by the atmosphere than when the sun is directly overhead. The sun's rays are weak, and the days are short and cold. It may be dark when you leave for school and dusk when you get home.

Seasons in the Southern Hemisphere are exactly opposite to seasons in the Northern Hemisphere. In June, when the South Pole leans away from the sun, it is winter in the Southern Hemisphere. People who live in Australia may head for the ski slopes in July and swim in the ocean on New Year's Day.

However, close to the equator in the tropics, the earth's tilt makes little difference. The length of tropical days and nights does not vary as much from winter to summer as it does in the Temperate Zone. You could participate in outdoor sports in the late afternoons during all seasons of the year. Throughout the year sunshine is more intense than in the Temperate Zone because at midday at the equator the sun is overhead. People who live in the Temperate Zones are sometimes unaware of this and return from tropical vacations with severe sunburns.

Winter temperatures in the tropics are the same as those in the summer. You could not build a snowman, have a snowball fight, go sledding or skating, follow animal tracks through a frosty whitened forest, or have to shovel snow, for in the tropics it never snows. Even in winter you would not need any ski pants, mittens, wool scarves, or heavy warm boots, but only your light summer clothes.

The *species* of plants and animals that live in any forest are determined by seasons. In a temperate forest living things must adapt to the extremes of winter cold and summer heat. In the summer the *canopy,* the green "roof" of the forest formed by the spreading leaves and branches of tall trees, provides cooling shade underneath. Birds nest in the smaller trees such as hawthorn and hazel that grow in the *understory,* the layer of the forest beneath the canopy. There they are protected from the hot summer sun and the sharp eyes of hawks, owls, and other hunting animals flying overhead.

The shrub layer of the temperate forest consists of the bushes such as huckleberry, blueberry, honeysuckle, and mountain laurel that grow below the understory. It is in the shrub layer that the large *mammals* of the forest such as deer, foxes, and bears find food and shelter.

The next time you walk through a forest notice the kinds of plants that make up the herb layer and live on the forest floor. You'll see wildflowers, ferns, mosses, and wild mushrooms. Small creatures such as worms, beetles, termites, grubs, and salamanders feed on the fallen leaves and rotting plants in the herb layer.

Also notice the soil in the temperate forest. It feels soft and spongy as you walk on it. This is because of the layers of slowly rotting leaves, pine needles, and other once-living things. As they decay, they form a soft bed of loamy, dark soil called *humus* that is rich in *nutrients.* Earthworms and minute creatures mix the humus into the soil, continually replenishing its nutrients.

Temperate forests usually contain less than twelve kinds of woody species, plants that have wood or wood fibers. Oak, ash, birch, pine, and beech are the five most common trees in temperate forests. Sometimes one species such as oak dominates and the forest is referred to as an "oak forest." A tropical forest, on the other hand, may have more than three hundred woody species within just two or three acres of land. Among the trees, only two or three may be the same species.

Tropical rain forests are the descendants of ancient forests that have existed on earth for millions of years. The glaciers that covered most of North America during the last Ice Age, depositing sand, gravel, boulders, and clay when they melted, did not extend as far south as the New World rain forests. The soil in these forests is hundreds of millions of years old.

The impression of modern visitors to undisturbed parts of the South American rain forest is similar to those of two nineteenth-century English explorers. Alfred Russel Wallace and Henry Walter Bates were friends who were keen observers of nature and began exploring the Amazon Basin together in 1848. Mr. Wallace spent four years in Brazil and Mr. Bates remained for eleven years. The region was almost unexplored by Europeans at the time. To support themselves Bates and Wallace collected plants and animals that they sold to private collectors and to the British Museum. They also wrote about the native people of the jungle who were their guides and about the strange plants and animals they saw on their travels.

Wallace and Bates described the rain forest's silence and a feeling of loneliness within it. In morning and evening they heard the terrifying roaring and then moaning sounds of howler monkeys, whose voices carry for several miles. The noontime stillness might be shattered by the sound of a large tree crashing in the forest, creating a light *gap* or opening where sunlight could penetrate the forest floor. The occasional piercing cries of animals attacking one another broke the silence. The native people attributed sounds they could not explain to *curupira,* the wild man or spirit of the forest.[1]

Since the explorations of Wallace and Bates almost a century and a half ago we have learned much more about the New World tropics. Temperature and rainfall are two ways we define a tropical forest. The intense tropical sunlight warms the air and causes water to evaporate. Tropical rain forests have high humidity and it rains almost every day for much of the year. While all forests are somewhat similar to a lake in that water evaporates from their surface, in a tropical rain forest more water evaporates because of the stronger sunlight and higher temperatures.

During the rainy season the morning sun warms the air, causing moisture to quickly evaporate from the leaves of trees and other forest plants. By midafternoon water vapor forms wisps of white clouds in the east. In a few hours the sky darkens, a strong wind sweeps through the forest, thunder

1. Barbara G. Beddall, ed., *Wallace and Bates in the Tropics* (London: The Macmillan Company, Collier-Macmillan, 1969) 35.

rumbles, and lightning flashes, and by early evening the dark storm clouds produce torrents of rain that pelt the canopy trees. When dawn breaks the sky is clear and the cycle begins again.

The high humidity in tropical rain forests causes the formation of clouds that produce afternoon thunderstorms and torrents of rain.

About half of the rainwater that falls on the forest rapidly evaporates back into the atmosphere. The rest drips through the understory, shrub, and herb layers. Only about 10 percent of the water actually reaches the forest floor. Humidity in the lower layers of the forest is therefore higher between downpours than is humidity in the canopy, where there is more direct sunlight to dry out the vegetation.

Some tropical plants have leaves with thin pointed ends called drip tips that are like spouts. They allow rainwater to run off the leaf quickly. Drip tips are advantageous to some plants because water does not remain on the leaf for a long time carrying nutrients away and preventing sunlight from reaching it.

The avocado is a plant that you can easily grow from seed to see the drip tips on its leaves. Holding the seed vertically so the pointed end is up, insert three or four toothpicks into the middle of the seed so that they protrude at right angles. Place the seed on top of a glass with the toothpicks resting on the glass's rim. Keep the glass filled with enough water so that it touches the bottom of the seed, and put the glass in a warm place with indirect sunlight. In about a month, when the root is touching the bottom of the glass, plant the seed in a pot, covering the bottom half of it with soil. Water it regularly and soon your plant will have many leaves with their characteristic drip tips.

A tropical moist rain forest looks like a dense green mass of tangled plants. In no other environment do plants grow so fast. Unlike a temperate forest, where temperatures change sharply and growth is seasonal, the rain forest is like a greenhouse with its warm, humid air year round. Rain forests have one of the most uniform temperatures on earth. The constant warmth and predictable rainfall provide ideal growing conditions. If you were to fly over the Amazonian rain forest in a small plane, it would resemble a vast green ocean.

The layers of a tropical rain forest blend in one tier to another because the vegetation is so lush. The tall canopy trees representing many different species all growing at different heights give the canopy its rolling, uneven appearance. *Saplings,* young trees, will grow into the canopy when mature, and shorter trees such as palms that can tolerate more shade live in the understory. The shrub and herb layers are often considered as one layer because many of the herb-layer plants are as tall as those in the shrub layer. Some climbing plants and vines occupy all the tiers of the rain forest.

The red sandy and clay soils of the tropical rain forest have practically no layer of decaying matter. The consistently high temperatures and humidity cause leaves and dead animals to decay rapidly and their nutrients are quickly reused by trees and other forest plants and animals. Because there is no winter in the tropics, the breakdown of dead materials occurs throughout the year. Therefore there is no buildup of humus as there is in temperate forests.

Every layer of the forest provides a different kind of *habitat* with variations in sunlight, temperature, and humidity. Unlike the temperate forests, where most animals live in the lower layers of the forest, in tropical rain forests more animals live in the canopy than in any other part.

The umbrella-shaped *crowns* of the very tallest trees, which are called *emergents,* emerge or poke through above the canopy. Emergent trees receive 100 percent sunlight and the canopy receives slightly less. The forest floor, however, receives only 2 to 3 percent of the sunlight that shines on the canopy. For this reason tropical rain forests are sometimes referred to as "closed forests" because the shade from the tree crowns prevents most light from reaching the forest floor. The floor is shaded, and many of the plants that live there have large leaves so they have more surface area to absorb the dim

Canopy trees tower above the rain forest like the green roof of a majestic cathedral, and beneath the ground is dimly lit.

light. There can be as much as a 10-degree difference in temperature between the canopy and the cooler forest floor.

Some visitors to the Amazonian rain forest compare the canopy to the roof of a great cathedral. It towers above, and beneath, the ground is dimly lit. The trunks of many tall rain forest trees are bare of branches until they reach the canopy. In order to appreciate the height of canopy trees, stand at the base of the tallest tree near where you live in the Temperate Zone. By imagining that you could put another tree the same height on top of it, you can get an idea of just how tall trees in the rain forest can grow. Canopy trees often reach heights of 120 to 150 feet and emergents can be 200 feet tall! A German scientist, Alexander von Humboldt, who spent from 1799 to 1804 exploring South American rain forests, described the Amazon as being a "forest above a forest."

The canopy is formed by the spreading leaves and branches of tall trees and by thick woody vines called *lianas.* Lianas include many kinds of climbing plants. Some are flat like ribbon, some are circular like string, and some are braided like rope. Lianas are flexible shoots that are rooted in the ground. They grow upward through the understory to the canopy in order to reach sunlight that is essential for their growth. There they become tangled in branches and other lianas, lacing together the canopy vegetation.

Lianas may grow hundreds of feet long and weigh as much as a ton. Using trees for support, they attach themselves with thorns, or by little roots that cling to cracks in the bark. They are one of the plants that give temperate visitors a feeling that the jungle has a hanging atmosphere. It is hard to distinguish the boundaries of one plant from another. Monkeys make their way through the jungle by swinging from one liana to another without ever touching the ground. Native people of the jungle make use of lianas' strength by building bridges of them across streams.

Besides lianas, other plants add to the weight of the trees' crowns. These are special kinds of plants that grow in the canopy where sunlight is plentiful. *Epiphytes* are plants such as orchids, ferns, mosses, lichens, and others, that grow piggyback on the high branches of trees. The word *epiphyte*

Lianas are rooted in the ground and grow upward through the understory to the canopy, becoming tangled in forest vegetation and lacing it together.

is derived from two Greek words—*epi* meaning upon and *phyton* meaning plant. Epiphyte therefore means "upon plants." The host tree provides the epiphyte with lodging but not with food. The epiphyte uses the tree for support, getting water from the rain. Sometimes it establishes its roots in a tree crevice where leaves have rotted. However, many epiphytes can make their only food from sunlight and the air.

Standing on the ground you cannot see the beautiful *aerial* gardens of epiphytes. Red, pink, purple, and other colorful flowers of the epiphytes look as if an artist has dabbed brilliant colors of paint against the dark green canopy. How do these plants reach the treetops? The *spores* of ferns are blown by the wind. The seeds of most other epiphytes are distributed by animals. Birds and bats deposit the seeds on the branches in their droppings. If a small amount of soil has been formed from rotting leaves on a branch, this is an ideal place for the seed to grow.

Bromeliads are kinds of epiphytes that are members of the pineapple family. They have thick, waxy leaves arranged in a circular cluster that forms a tank that catches and stores rainwater. Some bromeliad tanks can hold as much as two gallons of water. Bromeliads get their food from dead leaves and insects that fall into their water tanks and decay. Some frogs and insects live in these small "ponds."

Stranglers are plants such as figs that begin life in the same way as epiphytes. Their seeds are deposited on tree branches by birds or bats in their droppings or by the wind. After they have sprouted they send out long roots that dangle in the air and eventually anchor in the ground. The roots send water and nutrients back up to the plant, promoting its rapid growth. Over time the roots of the strangler multiply and almost completely surround the tree's trunk. They rob it of essential nutrients. Eventually the tree dies and decays, leaving the strangler to stand alone.

If you took a walk in a rain forest, you would notice that many of the tall trees have other strange-looking growths at their bases. Rain forest trees have slender trunks and their shallow roots give little support. In order to help the tree bear the weight of its heavy crown and not be toppled by a windy tropical storm, nature has supplied some of these trees with auxiliary roots. These roots are called "buttress roots" because they act like a buttress, a structure built against a wall to give support and strength. The flying buttresses of cathedrals, for example, are arched structures that extend beyond the side of the building to support it.

Buttress roots may have numerous shapes depending on the species of the tree. Plank buttress roots are triangular woody platelike projections. They begin about fifteen feet above the ground and look like wooden fins extending outward several feet from the trunk to the ground.

Stilt roots are slender, round buttress roots that extend from the trunks of some trees. The tree does not balance itself on these stilt roots as the clown balances on stilts in the circus. Rather, stilt roots grow downward from the trunk or branches around the tree's base. They support the tree and soak up nutrients and water from the soil. Scientists are puzzled why some tall rain forest trees develop buttress roots and others do not.

Many rain forest animals are as unusual in appearance as the plants. The keel-billed toucan is one of the strangest birds of the forest. It's bigger than a crow and its red-, yellow-, blue-, and black-striped bill looks as if mother nature got the beaks mixed up and it should be on a larger bird. Another unusual bird, the hoatzin, is about the size of a pigeon. The hoatzin resembles a feathered version of the prehistoric flying dinosaurs called coelurosaurs. It has an unpleasant smell and taste and is sometimes called the stinkbird. The hoatzin lives near streams, and when it is frightened it dives into the water and swims away. Jungle frogs are also unusual. Half of them do not live in ponds and streams as the frogs we are familiar with do, but high up in the trees. Some of these rain forest frogs such as the poison-arrow frog produce some of the strongest natural poisons in the world. Even many of the mammals are peculiar. Sloths are about the size of small dogs but with stubby snouts and tails. They spend their days hanging from a branch upside down and even eat and sleep in this position. One important reason for preserving the rain forest is to protect the many distinct forms of life that live only there.

Insects are a vital part of the rain forest. No one knows how many species of tropical insects exist. However, it is estimated that only about 10 percent of them even have names. Billions of beetles, termites, ants, and other insects feed on plants and dead animals, promoting their swift decay and helping to recycle their nutrients back into the soil. Ants are probably the most abundant insects and interact with all other plants and animals in the forest. They can have very complicated relationships within their own colonies.

One method some scientists have devised of studying the canopy insects is by "fogging." Before sunrise, when there is no wind, an *insecticide* is sprayed through a high-powered nozzle up into the canopy, creating a chemical "fog." This is poisonous to insects but apparently does not injure plants and other animals. The dead insects drop out of the trees onto sheets spread under the canopy. The insects are sorted and counted, and the data are entered on portable computers in the forest. The insects are then taken to museums for further sorting. The *biologists* can then identify and count the number of insects living in that part of the canopy. After a short period of time, the insecticide breaks down into harmless substances.

The huge assortment of plants that grow in the tropical rain forest is the reason so many species of animals also live there. However, as with plants, the number of animal species is very high but the number of individuals within any one species in a given area is very low. For example, when you walk in a temperate forest you are likely to see many gray squirrels scurrying about. However, in a tropical forest you are more likely to see many different species, but very few, perhaps only one, of each kind of animal.

Some animals grow to gigantic sizes compared with their Temperate Zone counterparts. The wingspan of a Morpho butterfly may be as wide as seven inches. Imagine meeting one-inch-long ants, five- to six-inch-long beetles, eight-inch-long slugs, and six-foot earthworms in the forest. The goliath frog is sixteen inches long, and the elephant shrew grows to twenty inches, bearing little resemblance to its tiny mouse-sized cousins that burrow in our backyards. Similarly, adult South American giant river otters are six feet long, gigantic relatives of the small, playful otters of the Temperate Zone.

The bird-eating spider is the largest spider in the world and the giant anaconda, which can measure thirty feet, is the longest snake.

With such an abundance of living things in the rain forest, you might expect to see monkeys swinging from branch to branch, glimpse a jaguar crouching in the underbrush, and spy exotic, colorful birds calling in the trees. Quite to the contrary, the animals are hard to find. The color green is everywhere, with little other color in sight. Many plants have large, shiny, leathery leaves that hide the colorful birds and animals. Rain forest animals blend in with the forest. This allows them either to hide from their enemies or to be more effective hunters. For example, the Latin American palm viper, which is a poisonous snake that eats birds, has a similar shape and color to the branch of a tree. Although the snake may be near you, you might not notice it.

Have you ever done one of those puzzles in a book or magazine where different objects are hidden in a picture and you have to find them? At first glance none of the objects is visible, but after a while, by studying the lines, you can find the different shapes. Finding animals in the rain forest is a similar activity.

The greatest concentration of species on earth is in the canopy of the tropical rain forest. Canopy birds include toucans, parakeets, parrots, birds of paradise, macaws, cockatoos, hornbills, and many others. Most canopy animals are *herbivorous,* meaning that they eat or survive on plants. Birds do not have to *migrate* because nuts, fruits, and flowers are plentiful year round. Some bats such as the fruit bat, the long-tongued bat, and the scary-looking Halloween bat feed on nectar or fruit. The latter has large ears, tiny eyes, and a gaping, toothy mouth. Leafhoppers are insects that hang upside down on the stem of a plant with their mouth parts piercing it. In this way they withdraw water and nutrients flowing from the plant's roots to its leaves.

Other birds, mammals, reptiles, *amphibians,* and insects are *carnivorous,* meaning that they feed on animals. Carnivorous birds such as the harpy eagle soar above the canopy and swoop down into the trees to capture a monkey or sloth in their strong claws. Some bats such as the vampire bat are carnivorous. They are smaller than the fruit-eating bats, which can have a two- to three-foot wingspan. Vampire bats use their sharp curved front teeth to puncture the skin of their victim, using their tongues to lick up the blood. Army ants are fierce carnivorous insects that travel in columns eating small creatures that do not escape the ants' advance in time. The blunthead tree snake eats lizards and the snail-eating snake's meals consist of slugs and snails. Piranhas are the savage carnivorous fish of Amazonian waters. Although they feed primarily on fish, they will attack other animals as well. Piranhas have protruding lower jaws and razor-sharp triangular teeth.

Whether plant- or meat-eating, animals must move through the forest to obtain food. The carnivorous crocodile and the herbivorous manatee, a large water-dwelling animal nicknamed the "sea cow," swim through the tropical waterways they inhabit. Anteaters, strange-looking creatures with long snouts and bushy tails, walk from one place to another in search of insect nests. When they find one, they rip it apart with their sharp claws and catch the frantic insects on their

Pictures of vampire bats are a common Halloween symbol but these mammals actually live in the New World tropics.

sticky tongues. Birds, bats, and some kinds of insects fly through the rain forest. Jaguars, monkeys, lizards, frogs, sloths, and other animals climb to sources of food. Still other animals such as snakes glide through the canopy, almost as if they were swimming through the trees.

People have inhabited the Amazonian rain forest for at least ten thousand years. These native forest dwellers, generally called Indians, live in harmony with its plants and animals. The lack of roads into the rain forest kept them isolated from the modern world. Tribes such as the Wayana Indians

The anole lizard.

who live on the northern coast of South America, the Yanomami of northern Brazil, and the Cayapo of eastern Brazil have an extensive knowledge of rain forest plants and animals. They have used these resources wisely for centuries without harming them. By hunting, trapping, and fishing, forest dwellers obtain food that keeps them well fed and healthy. They know how to hunt silently with arrows made from the stems of palm trees and tipped with the poison from the skin of the poison-arrow frog and blown through hollow reeds called *blowguns.*

They know which plants are good to eat, which can be used as medicines, and which are poisonous. Long before doctors discovered that the white salt from the cinchona tree could be used to treat malaria, the Indians were aware of its healing properties. They weave cotton into hammocks for sleeping and make baskets out of straw for carrying infants and food.

Indians use large tree trunks as structural supports in their huts and make roofs out of thatched palm leaves held together with creeping vines. There is no plumbing, so they fetch water from nearby streams. They wear feathers of colorful tropical birds for jewelry and use stems of a particular palm tree to make a musical instrument resembling a bassoon. There are no schools nearby and most children, like their parents, do not know how to read, but are taught how to live in the rain forest and use its resources to meet their

During the rainy season some children who live in flooded areas of the Amazon depend on a boat to travel from one place to another. This hollow log canoe is made from a ceiba tree.

basic needs. These primitive people have a deep respect for the land from which they get everything they need to live satisfying lives.

Native tribes grow crops in the forest in a kind of agriculture called "shifting cultivation." To *cultivate* means to prepare land for the raising of crops. You may know about the rotation of crops, or planting of different crops on the same land in alternate years, which is often done in the United States to keep the soil fertile. Shifting cultivation, however, means that the fields rather than the crops are rotated. Indians first clear one small patch of rain forest, which they cultivate, and then another. They use *machetes* to hack a clearing in the jungle. Once the foliage wilts, they set fire to the cleared land. This method is called "slash and burn." When the burned land cools, the Indians plant among the tree stumps and ashes a few crops that the family will need for survival. After a couple of years, when the soil becomes unsuitable for planting, the family moves to a new plot of land in the forest and begins again.

Because the cleared areas are so small, they will be naturally reforested. The plants that grow close to the ground grow back first and provide nutrients for saplings. If the abandoned land is left fallow for at least ten years, it will be completely reforested. For this reason, slash-and-burn agriculture on a small scale like that of the Indians is a sustainable use of the rain forest. It does not use it up faster than nature can renew it.

This type of farming is a form of subsistence farming. The word *subsist* means to have the minimum that is necessary to live. Through shifting cultivation and slash-and-burn ag-

In slash-and-burn agriculture the forest is set on fire. When it cools, Indians and settlers plant crops among the tree stumps and ashes.

riculture, Indians provide shelter and enough food for themselves and their families without causing permanent damage to the forest.

However, in the last forty-five years, following the end of World War II, human beings have brought great change to the rain forest. More and more of the primary forest, with its mature canopy trees, is being destroyed. Roads have been built into the forest so that minerals such as copper, tin, and gold can be mined, trees can be cut for lumber, cash crops such as bananas and coffee can be planted, and pasture can be created for cattle ranching. When people greatly alter large tracts of the rain forest, the secondary forest that grows in its place is so different that it is no longer suitable for many of the native species that previously lived there.

Plants and animals have adapted to a particular *environment* over millions of years, and abrupt change means many of them will die. Imagine a bird, such as the wood thrush of the temperate forest, migrating to its familiar patch of rain forest in Mexico every winter. If the wood thrush finds the forest has been cut, it becomes a wanderer and may die. Some prominent biologists believe that one species becomes extinct every day because of jungle deforestation.

Scientists do not know what caused the last great loss of species sixty-five million years ago. Half of all the plants and animals, including the dinosaurs, vanished from the face of the earth. This huge loss of life was due to a natural occurrence such as the impact of a giant meteor from space or extreme weather conditions. However, it's no mystery why so many species are becoming *extinct* (no longer existing) today. It is because of the activities of human beings.

No matter where you live in the world you are connected to the rain forest. Half of American songbirds winter in the New World tropics. The rain forests with their constant cloud cover create rainfall in the Northern Hemisphere and stabilize climate. Many of the medicines at your local pharmacy are derived from tropical plants. Even chocolate comes from a tropical tree.

As people we make huge demands on the resources of our planet. In doing this there are consequences for all living things. The fabric of life is composed of an interdependence of plants and animals that is only partially understood. Many species that live in the rain forest may be extinct before they have even been identified and given a name. Some may be essential for our own survival. For example, so far at least 1,400 varieties of tropical plants are thought to be potential cures for cancer.

Around the world more and more people are joining together to save the rain forests. While they speak many different languages, their urgent message is being heard and the results of their work are already evident. For example, some Central and South American countries are realizing the rain forests are more valuable preserved than destroyed. They are setting aside land as national parks and promoting natural history tours. In Japan restaurants are beginning to use chopsticks that are washed and reused rather than disposable chopsticks made from tropical woods. Most fast-food chains no longer buy Central American beef for hamburgers.

By reading this book and others about the rain forest you are becoming informed. The second step is to share what you've learned with others. Today start a journal titled "Jungle Rescue" in which you collect articles about the rain forest and develop your own action plan. Throughout this book there will be suggestions for steps you might take to inform classmates and people in your community. You will also read about the important work of scientists, some of whom became interested in the world of the rain forest as children. No matter where we live, each one of us has a special role to play in this jungle rescue.

2
Plant and Animal Partnerships

When you hear the word *community* you probably think of a group of people who live together in the same place or have common interests. Your city or town with its houses, stores, schools, places of worship, and industries is a community. Biologists, however, use the word community to include all the living things in a particular area. One of the main features of a biological community is the intricate way living things relate to one another.

Each species plays an important role in the community. Green plants are the producers. You never see a plant eating because they are food factories themselves. Green plants have tiny pores that let in light. In a process called *photosynthesis,* which means "putting together with light," plants change the radiant energy of the sun into food stored in their roots, stems, leaves, and seeds. In carrots food is stored in the roots, in celery in the stems, in lettuce in the leaves, and in corn in the seeds.

The amount of photosynthesis that occurs depends on the amount of sun and rain in a given area. In the tropical rain forest, where green plants are abundant, more photosynthesis occurs than anyplace else on earth. There is also a tremendous variety of plants and animals that live there. On the other hand, fewer plants and animals live in the desert, where there is very little photosynthesis.

Consumers such as people and other animals depend on green plants, or other living things that have fed on green plants, for food. This flow of energy in nature from one living thing to another is called a "food chain." The vegetation of any forest is the basis for nutrition that gets passed on from one animal to the next in the food chain. For example, at dusk great numbers of fruit-eating bats flutter through the canopy chomping a feast of ripe figs. All of this activity attracts the attention of hungry mottled owls, which silently swoop down to capture the bats for their meals.

Decomposers such as *bacteria, fungi,* ants, earthworms, slugs, and some insects obtain food by breaking down dead plants and animals. They are nature's recyclers. Decomposers return nutrients and minerals to the soil where plants take them up through their roots and use them to grow. When a tree falls in the rain forest large insects such as beetles bore into the wood. Then ants, and eventually termites, use the rotting wood for their tunnels. The wood becomes soft and moist and fungi grow. Eventually bacteria, one-celled organisms that are so tiny they can be seen only with a microscope, reduce the decaying material into parts so small they dissolve into the soil.

In a tropical rain forest the high humidity, great numbers of decomposers, and rapid growth of plants promote the quick recycling of nutrients from the soil back to the vegetation. Therefore, if the trees are cut down for logging, most of their nutrients are also transported out of the forest. Unlike temperate forests there is little humus.

In the forest community living things relate to each other in three major ways: *predation, symbiosis,* and *competition.* Predation is the behavior of capturing, killing, and feeding on other animals. The animal that lives in this way is called the *predator* and the animal that is hunted or killed is called the *prey.*

Predator-prey relationships help to maintain the natural order of the rain forest. Jaguars, large members of the cat family with big heads and short golden fur with black spots, reign supreme in the South American jungle. Their prey includes tapirs, relatives of the horse and rhinoceros; peccaries, animals like wild pigs; brocket deer; and agouti, rodents about the size of a rabbit. Jaguars are well suited for predation. They can climb trees, catch fish with their paws, and swim after tapirs, which like to wallow in the mud of shallow water to rid themselves of insects.

In order to reduce their chances of being eaten, many animals have developed ways of making themselves appear less appetizing. One of these is called *mimicry.* You might mimic someone else by imitating the way that person looks, acts, or speaks. But in nature, mimicry is the way one living thing has developed over thousands of years to resemble something else. In this way, it is able to protect itself from its predators. Certain spiders that are good food resemble sharp-spined ants, and some species of katydids, large green grasshoppers, look like finely veined green leaves. Many species of birds like to eat butterflies just as much as you like ice cream. You might prefer one flavor to another but basically it all tastes good. This is not the case for birds with butterflies on their menus. Some butterflies are delicious, some taste awful, and some are actually poisonous. Some of the nonpoisonous species mimic the bad-tasting ones by having developed similar colors and markings on their wings. A predator, having tried the unpleasant-tasting variety, will remember its appearance and avoid it in the future.

Camouflage, which is a disguise or false appearance that is used to hide something, is used by both plants and animals so they do not become another's meal. The sloth's disguise helps it to avoid being spotted by predators, such as the harpy eagle. The coarse hairs of the sloth's fur have grooves in which *algae,* one-celled plants that do not have roots or flowers, grow. The algae give the fur a greenish tinge, enabling the sloth to blend in with the forest plants and be less visible to the eagle as it hunts through the canopy. The boa constrictor, a very large nonpoisonous snake that kills other animals by coiling itself around them, is itself protected from becoming prey by its coloration. The dark spots and blotches on this brown snake are an effective camouflage.

The bright colors of some other animals attract attention to them and signify that they are dangerous. The poison-arrow frog's scarlet body warns other animals to stay away.

The slow-moving sloth is well camouflaged because the green algae that live on its gray fur make it blend in with the forest.

Shield bugs have bright red shield-shaped backs that announce that they are dangerous to eat.

Symbiosis is the living together in close association of two different kinds of organisms. A symbiotic relationship that occurs in the rain forest can also be observed in practically any garden. As bees and hummingbirds drink nectar, the sweet sugary water of the flower, they become smeared with pollen. *Pollen* is the mass of fine grains resembling yellow dust found inside the flower. *Pollination* is the transfer of pollen from the male to the female part of the flower. When this happens, *fertilization* occurs. The flower's petals wilt and the fruit of the plant, which contains the plant's seeds, begins to grow.

In temperate forests pollination occurs in large measure by the wind. The blossoms of trees in these forests are not large and colorful, and you may not even notice that they are in bloom. Many trees such as willow, birch, and alder have catkins. These are flower clusters growing in circular rows along a slender stalk, which hang down like fuzzy fingers from branches of the tree. Catkins contain pollen and are carried from one tree to another on the wind. In temperate forests seeds as well as pollen are carried by the wind. You are probably familiar with maple keys, the fruits of the maple tree that have two wings and float on the wind.

In the rain forests, however, animals are the chief pollinators. This symbiotic plant-animal relationship is a key part of the forests' growth and survival. In such a sea of green, how do animal pollinators find the flowers? Bees and other insects are attracted to their fragrance and bright blossoms. Even some large emergent trees, when in bloom, are beautiful shades of red, yellow, and purple. The feathers of such hummingbirds as the fork-tailed plumeteer become dusted with pollen when they are drinking the flowers' nectar. Small mammals such as bats get pollen on their tongues. When they fly out of the flower they carry the pollen with them. Birds also ensure the continuation of the forest by depositing seeds in their wastes. Scientists are still studying the extent of these important symbiotic relationships

Symbiotic relationships can be *mutual,* in which both species benefit, *commensal,* in which one species benefits and the other is not affected, or *parasitic,* in which one species benefits and the other is harmed. Examples of these exist in your backyard or neighborhood park. Mutualism exists between some species of trees and birds. The tree provides a nesting site and food for the bird, and the bird disperses the tree's seeds in its droppings after eating the fruit. However, if you sit under the tree on a hot summer day, benefiting from the shade of its branches, your relationship with the tree is commensal because the tree is unaffected by your presence. But if the tree's leaves are eaten by gypsy moth caterpillars, weakening the tree because it is less able to perform photosynthesis, the relationship between the tree and the caterpillars is parasitic.

Some of the symbiotic relationships that exist in the rain forest have no counterparts in the Temperate Zone. One example of mutualism is the relationship between leaf-cutter ants and a grayish white fungus called *Rhozites gonglyophora.* Leaf-cutting ants create pathways through the jungle understory as columns of ants strip the foliage bare. Ants surge up tree trunks and vines and along branches, cutting leaves into pieces that they carry on their backs to their underground nest. There other leaf-cutting ants chew the leaves and plant the pulp with the fungus. The fungus feeds on the leaf pulp and produces a liquid that is the ants' food. Without this symbiotic relationship neither the fungus nor the ants could survive.

Army ants and antbirds are examples of a commensal symbiotic relationship. Army ants march in columns, either single file or up to twelve feet wide, depending on the species. The sound of so many ants moving through dead leaves on the forest floor makes a distinctive rattle, a sound dreaded by other animals, which desperately try to escape the ants' advance. Snakes, birds, frogs, lizards, grasshoppers, moths, beetles, and small mammals frantically rush for cover. Antbirds hover above the army ants and eat the insects that they flushed out of the vegetation on the forest floor. The army ants are not helped or harmed by their relationship with the antbirds.

Army ants moving in columns through the dead leaves on the ground make a distinctive rattle, a sound dreaded by other animals.

Plants can also have commensal relationships. Orchids, bromeliads, and other kinds of epiphytes that grow high up in the canopy have a commensal relationship with the rain forest tree on whose limbs they grow. These lofty branches support the epiphytes high above the ground, where light conditions are favorable for their growth. Unless the weight of these plants becomes so heavy that the tree is weakened, the tree neither benefits nor is harmed by their presence.

If you have a dog that has ever gotten a tick on its fur, then you are familiar with parasitism. The tick, or parasite, gets nourishment from the blood meal provided by your dog, the host. The dog begins to itch, feel uncomfortable, and may even get sick as a result of being bitten by the tick. Parasites are usually much smaller than their hosts and unlike predators do not kill them and eat them immediately but feed over a long time. In the tropics parasites are everywhere. They may live as some worms do in the intestines of their hosts, or they may attach to the host's skin.

The third major way living things relate to each other is competition. You might think of competition as an athletic event where one individual or team tries to win over another, or as a contest for a prize. However, in a biological community, living things compete for limited resources. To survive, animals need food, water, and shelter from enemies. Perhaps you have seen birds competing for food at a backyard feeder. A bird that is eating at the feeder may move away when a larger or more forceful bird arrives. Both birds are competing for the limited resource, the seeds in the feeder. The bird that has the greatest chance of survival is the one that is most successful in getting the seed. Competition can occur between members of the same species (two chickadees struggling for control of the feeder) or between different species (a chickadee and a blue jay confronting each other at the feeder). Rarely does competition involve direct fighting. It is more commonly limited to threatening behavior such as the birds flapping their wings and attempting to peck each other.

Competition also exists among plants. They compete for a space to grow, sunlight, water, and nutrients in the soil. When seedlings are planted close together, they compete for water and nutrients in a limited space. The gardener or farmer thins the plants, by pulling some of them out, to reduce competition. Weeds also compete with flowers or vegetables in the garden.

In the rain forest the loud voices of howler monkeys heard during the morning hours warn their competitors to stay away from their home range. This behavior lessens fighting for mates and resulting injuries. By declaring a territory theirs, howler monkeys also ensure that the number of mon-

The voice of the black howler monkey can be heard for miles.

keys does not become so great in any one area that there is not enough food available. There is competition not only for food, but for good places to rest and sleep, and for observation posts.

Monkeys also compete with human beings for resources of the rain forest. When trees are cut down for timber or the forest is cleared for farming or cattle ranching, monkeys can no longer drink the sweet nectar of rain forest flowers and eat the fruit of the trees. Without question, the most important factor in the decreasing number of New World monkeys is the far-reaching effects of deforestation caused by people. As acres of primary rain forest are burned and bulldozed, more and more kinds of monkeys become *endangered species.* An endangered species is one in which the number of animals is so low that it is in danger of becoming extinct.

The particular division of the animal kingdom into which monkeys are classified is called the *primate* group. There are 227 species of primates including lemurs, monkeys, apes, and human beings. Primates are a group of mammals many of which have the following characteristics. They are more dependent on their sense of sight than on their sense of smell. Usually they live in groups and form social relationships with each other, and their infants are very dependent on their mothers. Most primates have flexible hands and feet, which usually each have five fingers and toes that can be used for grasping. Instead of the claws that many animals have, primates generally have at least some nails at the ends of their fingers and toes.

Primates are divided into two main groups. We are much less familiar with the group called prosimians. They are found in the Old World tropics of Africa and Asia and include many small *nocturnal* creatures as well as lemurs. Lemurs are furry creatures with long fluffy tails that live on Madagascar and the Comoro Islands, both of which are off the coast of Africa.

The other group of primates, the simians, includes many species with which you are familiar. Simians are found in both the New and Old World tropics and include most monkeys you see at the zoo, apes, and human beings. Apes, including gibbons, orangutans, gorillas, and chimpanzees, are found only in the Old World tropics. They have no tails and are generally larger and more intelligent than monkeys. Perhaps you have read about Dian Fossey or seen the movie *Gorillas in the Mist,* which told the story of Dian's work to save the mountain gorillas in Africa. Another woman, Jane Goodall, is currently studying the behavior of and trying to save another type of African ape, the chimpanzee.

South American children who live in rural forested areas are so accustomed to seeing monkeys in the trees that they find it surprising to learn that there are no monkeys living in our temperate forests. In fact, no monkeys live in the wild in North America, north of Mexico. However, you can see and learn about lots of different kinds of monkeys by visiting a zoo.

When you go to the zoo find the primate section. Read the signs identifying each species of monkey and where it is found in the wild. New World monkeys, as compared with Old World monkeys, are fairly small and live in trees, spending very little time on the ground. The pygmy marmoset weighs less than four and a half ounces and is the smallest monkey in the New World. Night monkeys have faces resembling owls, and are the only nocturnal monkeys in the world. Sakis are a kind of monkey that can leap as much as thirty feet and sometimes are called "flying monkeys." Notice their large, thick tails. Cotton-top tamarins are tiny monkeys with pug noses, black faces, and a thatch of white hair that sticks straight up on their heads.

When you observe monkeys you often see them grooming each other, using their teeth and fingers to remove insect eggs from the fur. Along with providing important social relationships, this prevents pests from hatching and burrowing under the skin, causing discomfort and disease.

When animals are raised in captivity, they do not have to forage for food or develop the skills that enable them to survive in the wild. Therefore, trying to save endangered species in captive breeding programs at zoos is a last-ditch effort compared with maintaining their numbers in the wild. Many zoological gardens, recognizing that caged primates are unhappy in such a confined environment, are constructing artificial rain forests more similar to the animals' natural habitat.

One monkey you are very likely to see at the zoo is the capuchin, the most common New World primate. In the South American jungles, capuchins seem to belong to groups which occupy certain territories. During the mornings and late afternoons, they travel through the forest searching for flowers and fruit to eat. If branches are too far apart for a young monkey to reach, a female adult makes a "monkey bridge," stretching her body between the branches so the little monkey can make its way across.

At night capuchins join with several other of their species to sleep in small groups in the trees. Although many South American monkeys stay mainly in the canopy, capuchins travel throughout the levels of the jungle and often come to the forest floor to get water from streams and rivers. Capuchins are the most intelligent of all monkeys and are the kind of monkey you may have seen perform in circuses.

One monkey you won't see in a circus or zoo is the muriqui, which does not survive well in captivity. The muriqui is South America's largest monkey. Adult monkeys of this species can weigh thirty-five pounds and can measure five feet in length. Muriquis are mischievous and merry, liking to play

Scientists are hoping to save the muriqui, South America's largest monkey, from extinction. The muriqui population has dropped to about four hundred and they do not survive well in zoos.

by chasing and wrestling each other. Like some other New World monkeys, the muriqui has a long strong tail called a *prehensile* tail. It has an area of bare skin at the end of it which can be used for grasping or for hanging.

The muriqui is an endangered species and scientists believe that only four hundred of these monkeys survive. By studying them in the wild scientists are learning more about their behavior in the hope of saving them from extinction. One of the scientists studying the muriqui is Dr. Karen Strier, a faculty member at the University of Wisconsin in Madison. As a child she was always interested in the behavior of people and animals and liked being out of doors. When she was a junior in college, she assisted in a project studying baboons in the African grassland called a savanna. This was such a meaningful experience that she later enrolled in graduate school at Harvard University to further study primates. She was also eager to learn more about a variety of primates in their natural habitats.

Dr. Strier is presently directing a project gathering information about the muriqui and how it relates to its environment. With the help of Brazilian graduate students, she watches these monkeys and records their activities, their location in the forest, and the distance between them and others of the same species. Dr. Strier is able to distinguish individual muriquis because of their natural markings, and has given them names. For example, she might observe, "Nancy is feeding on ripe fruit of tree species no. 768 with her infant in contact, dorsal [on the back], less than two meters from Mona." She actually writes this in codes so that the information can be written rapidly. Family records of births have been kept since 1982 and in many cases scientists know who the young monkey's mother is and who the father may be as well.

In addition to observing the monkeys, scientists also monitor the vegetation. In this way they can determine what foods are available for the monkeys to eat, and what they actually select. It is as if an observer watched you go through a cafeteria line, writing down all the foods from which you could choose, and then recording what you actually put on your tray and ate. In the rain forest, where there is such a variety of plants available for the monkeys to eat, scientists have worked out an intricate system of monitoring the vegetation to ensure their data is accurate.

Dr. Strier says: "If you were an assistant helping me, you would need to wake up early in the morning between 4:30 A.M. and 6:00 A.M. depending on the season in order to get to the monkeys before they wake up and leave the area where they slept. You would follow the monkeys around, climbing up and down hills while they swing through the trees, trying not to lose sight of the monkeys' movements, activities, and social relationships. You would also be marking the trees that they feed in with plastic colored flagging tape, and trying to collect samples of what they eat so you could identify it later. You would stay with the monkeys for the entire day, until they settle down again for the night in another part of the forest. This would be anytime between about 5:00 P.M. and 7:00 P.M., again depending on the season. (They wake up earlier and stay active longer during the Brazilian summer months than during the winter.)

"Once the monkeys were settled down, you would return to

The poison-arrow frog's bright scarlet color warns other animals to keep away. This frog produces one of the strongest natural poisons in the world.

One way of clearing the forest is to set fire to an area. These wildfires often rage out of control.

Bromeliads are kinds of epiphytes that are members of the pineapple family.

Leaf-cutter ants trim leaves off nearby plants and carry them to huge underground nests.

The birds of the tropical rain forest such as the macaw are some of the most vividly colored in the world.

The jaguar, weighing between 125 and 250 pounds, is the largest of the New World cats.

The toucan is a canopy bird with an oversized bill.

A program to breed the golden lion tamarin in captivity and return the zoo-born animals to the wild is helping to save this endangered species of monkey.

the research house at the entrance to the forest. The house has two bedrooms, a kitchen, and a bathroom. Water for hot showers is piped from a stream in the forest into a tank where the wood-burning fire can heat it. There is no electricity; after dark the only source of light is from gas lamps."[2]

Of the 227 species of primates, forty-eight, or one in five, are endangered and the low numbers of many others are of great concern. In addition to the muriqui, many other endangered primates are found only in the New World tropics. The golden lion tamarin lives in the state of Rio de Janeiro and the black lion tamarin, whose numbers are now less than a hundred, lives in São Paulo which, like Rio de Janeiro, is part of Brazil. The Peruvian yellow-tailed woolly lives in the cloud forests of northern Peru and the cotton-top tamarin is a resident of Colombia.

By destroying the rain forest, killing monkeys for food, and capturing them for pets and other uses, people are responsible for the growing number of endangered South American primates. Primates are hunted in all the New World tropics in which they are found. For some tribes the meat from these animals is an important source of protein in the diet. For centuries tropical forest dwellers in the Amazon have hunted monkeys for food with blowguns and bows and arrows. At one time the number of monkeys killed was so low that enough monkeys were born each year to replace those that were hunted.

As rain forest areas have become developed and nearby

2. Quoted with permission of Karen B. Strier, Ph.D., Department of Anthropology, University of Wisconsin at Madison.

cities have grown, more monkeys are being hunted. In some overhunted areas, there are large tracts of land in which certain species no longer exist. In many countries primates are legally protected, but laws are difficult to enforce in remote areas. Modern hunters use shotguns to shoot the monkeys, and the meat is no longer used only for the local tribes; it is used to supply city markets. Although we would consider eating monkey meat alien, for many people who live in or near jungles, it is considered a delicacy and is a favorite food.

In some Indian tribes, monkeys are believed to have healing properties and are hunted for their medicinal value. For example, in Costa Rica some tribes believe that rubbing monkey fat on your chest will help to cure a cold or pneumonia. If you were an Amazonian Indian child in Peru who had a cough, a killed howler monkey might be part of your cure. Its hair would be ground up and then put in boiling water. When the mixture was cool, you would drink it!

In addition to being captured for food and medicine, primates are also hunted for other reasons. Sometimes they are hunted for sport. Even some children use slingshots or air rifles to practice their marksmanship using monkeys as targets. While North American hunters may display the antlers or the stuffed head of a deer, hunters in the Amazon may make hats, rugs, and wall hangings out of monkey fur. Stuffed monkeys and necklaces of monkey teeth or bones and other monkey products are also for sale in tropical markets.

In the 1950s and 1960s the United States and other industrialized nations such as Japan and those in Western Europe have greatly contributed to simians' decline in another way. Primates, because they are the animals most like people, are used extensively in medical research. It is estimated that in the 1950s nearly one and a half million Old World monkeys were imported for use in medical laboratories where the polio vaccine was being developed. Today many new vaccines, medicines, and treatments are still tested on monkeys to see if they are safe and effective before they are approved for use on human beings.

The large drop in the number of primates worldwide and stricter government regulations mean that fewer monkeys are now taken from the wild for research purposes. Animal protection groups argue that the use of primates in medical research should be eliminated altogether or at least limited to those that are *bred* in captivity.

In addition to research, in past years large numbers of primates were exported as part of the pet trade. Many infant monkeys, taken from their mothers, which were shot for food, died on the way to their new surroundings. Others ended up in the hands of people who wanted an exotic pet but knew little about its needs and how to care for it. While it is not uncommon to see pet monkeys in the tropics, you won't see monkeys for sale in your local pet store. This is because in the mid-1970s the United States, along with many other nations, banned trade in primates. Monkeys can still be imported, however, by medical laboratories and qualified collectors such as zoos.

While live capture and hunting have contributed to the increasing disappearance of South American monkeys from the rain forests, these small lively animals have suffered most from loss of habitat. Worldwide, two-thirds of all nonhuman primates live in the wild in just four countries: Brazil, Zaire,

Indonesia, and Madagascar. Of these, Brazil has the most species within its borders and is therefore an extremely important country for primate *conservation.* Conservation means the careful preservation and protection of something. Primate conservation projects determine what actions are necessary to ensure the survival of primates in the wild.

Dr. Russell A. Mittermeier is a primate specialist who created the World Wildlife Fund Primate Program in 1979. As a child attending school in the Bronx and growing up on Long Island, New York, he read all the Tarzan books by Edgar Rice Burroughs and was captivated by life in the rain forest. He made frequent trips with his mother to the Bronx Zoo and the American Museum of National History. Russell was a keen observer of animals, loved the out of doors, and collected snakes and turtles from nearby ponds and woodlands which

Dr. Russell Mittermeier shows a primate poster to children in their village near the Brazil-Suriname border.

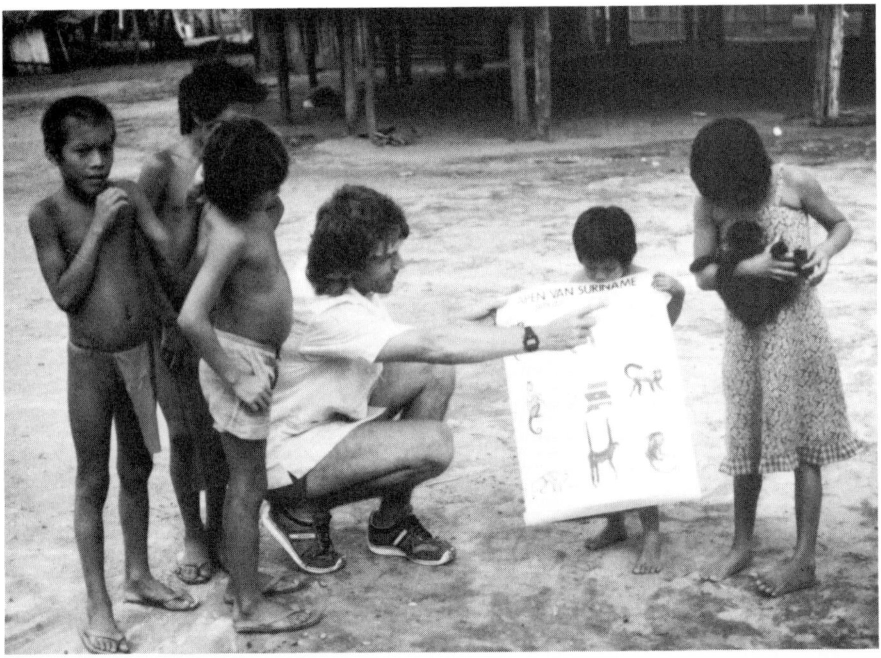

he kept in a homemade backyard pool. Graduating with honors from Dartmouth College, he went on to earn a Ph.D. from Harvard University.

As a wildlife biologist and teacher at the State University of New York at Stony Brook, Professor Mittermeier spends several months of the year studying primates in the wild. He is adept at climbing tall canopy trees to obtain samples of the food that monkeys eat, speaks seven languages fluently, and is as much at home hacking his way through the jungle as lecturing to a class. One of the foremost authorities on tropical rain forests and an international leader in saving endangered species of monkeys, Dr. Mittermeier is also president of Conservation International.[3]

Influenced by Dr. Mittermeier's work with primates, World Wildlife Fund and Smithsonian scientists in the United States, together with colleagues in Brazil and throughout the world, have established the Golden Lion Tamarin Project. The golden lion tamarin is a squirrel-sized monkey with beautiful golden hair that forms a mane around its face. These monkeys live in families in the rain forest and find shelter in old hollow trees that have openings that are too narrow to admit predators. Each family uses several trees and chooses one in which to spend the night depending on where it is that afternoon. For years, the tamarin family may use the same hollows, which become lined with their golden hair. Scientists estimate that each group of tamarins needs about 123 acres (fifty

3. Included with permission of Russell A. Mittermeier, Ph.D., Department of Anatomical Sciences, State University of New York at Stony Brook.

hectares) of rain forest to find enough fruit, insects, spiders, birds' eggs, and lizards to eat.

These monkeys have lived for centuries in a portion of the large rain forest which stretched inland along the Atlantic coast of Brazil. Now, less than 2 percent of these original forests remain. They have been reduced to a few isolated patches among large sprawling cities, rice and fruit farms, and cattle pastures.

The conservation program seeks to protect remaining habitats in Brazil, to increase the number of golden lion tamarins through a captive breeding program, and to educate local people about these primates and the rain forest. In 1974 a 12,844-acre (5,200-hectare) wildlife sanctuary, the Poço das Antas Federal Biological Reserve, was established in the Brazilian state of Rio de Janeiro. However, it now contains as many golden lion tamarins as it can support, and competition from people continues to undermine the reserve. Twenty-five percent of the reserve was converted to pasture and needs to be reforested to support the tamarins. Trains run through the reserve and disturb the animals and a recently completed dam may flood up to one-fifth of it. The last remaining stretches of forest outside the reserve are owned by ranchers and farmers who could cut them down at any time.

The second part of the conservation program is the captive breeding program and returning the zoo-born animals to the wild. In the early 1970s the National Zoological Park (National Zoo) in Washington, D.C., began a research program studying what golden lion tamarins needed in order to be healthy, form family relationships with each other, and breed in captivity. The program is successful, and so many animals of this species have been born and raised at this zoo, and at one hundred others around the world, that they now outnumber the remaining four hundred individuals that survive in the wild. If you visit the National Zoo and many other zoos, you can see golden lion tamarins.

A program is now underway to reintroduce these animals to the Atlantic rain forests of Brazil. Golden lion tamarins, after leaving their zoos, spend several months in the forest near Rio de Janeiro learning how to live in the wild. They progress from learning how to peel bananas left in plain view on the feeding platform to having to search for food and water their caretakers have hidden in hollow logs and other places where they would be found in the forest. Finally they become skilled at capturing food such as insects, lizards, and frogs that are capable of escape. They also learn how to find their way in the forest and to find shelter. The tamarins know instinctively that low-flying birds can be dangerous and make a distinctive chirp when they are around. Between 1984, when the project began, and the end of 1989, seventy-one golden lion tamarins were reintroduced into the wild. Of those, only twenty-seven now survive. Twenty-six infants were born to reintroduced animals and twenty-one of them are now living. This makes a total of forty-eight animals living in the forest as a result of the conservation program.

The third part of the conservation program is the education of local people and the training of Brazilian biologists. Before the education program was begun most residents were unaware of the existence of the Poço das Antas Federal Biological Reserve and of laws prohibiting hunting, capturing, and keeping golden lion tamarins as pets. They did not realize that destruction of the rain forest was pushing the tamarins and many other species of plants and animals to the brink of extinction.

Brazilian graduate students, community leaders, and volunteers have carried out many activities to teach how the well-being of people, the rain forest, and wildlife are all related. Young people have organized conservation clubs that help in the reserve and assist with community education projects. Students produced a play about golden lion tamarins, dressed up as golden lion tamarins for a parade, and organized field trips to the reserve. The golden lion tamarin has become a symbol of rescuing the rain forest for these people.[4]

Conservation leaders in Brazil give lectures to farmers, teachers, and local officials about conservation of the golden lion tamarin, and enlist their help. Biologists working with the World Wildlife Fund have asked landowners near the Poço das Antas Reserve to allow tamarins on their property. The owners agree to preserve the forest on their private lands. Many of these Brazilian hosts have become very concerned about the tamarin families and often help researchers monitor the animals' progress. They now realize the forest provides necessary habitat for the tamarins as well as helps to retain water sources on their land.

The conservation of primates is one part of the conservation of tropical rain forests. As we learn more about other

4. Information on the Golden Lion Tamarin Project is included with permission of Lou Ann Dietz, Brazil Program Officer, World Wildlife Fund.

species and view ourselves as fellow travelers on the planet earth with all other creatures, then there is every reason to hope the fragile, complex web of life that is the rain forest will be saved.

Two children dressed as golden lion tamarins in a parade devoted to the monkey and its newly established reserve

3
Riches of the Tropical Rain Forest

In many Central and South American countries the majority of people have a very low standard of living, meaning that they have few of the comforts of everyday life that most people in the United States take for granted. Many families live in small crowded huts with dirt floors, with no indoor plumbing or electricity, and without enough money for food or for medical care if illness strikes.

In Brazil the government regarded the Amazon rain forest with its vast acres of undeveloped land as a means for its poor citizens living in crowded city slums and impoverished rural areas to make a living by clearing the land, farming, and cattle raising. In the 1960s the government committed itself to a plan, called Operation Amazonia, to develop the Amazon region.

In addition to providing a solution to poverty and overcrowding, the government realized that there were vast quantities of timber and other natural resources that could be taken from the Amazon area and sold, helping to pay back money Brazil had borrowed from other nations. Another major consideration was that the Brazilian government worried that the wealth of mineral and timber resources would attract colonists from neighboring countries such as Peru and Venezuela to this sparsely populated area.

Prior to the 1960s the Amazon region was practically cut off from the rest of Brazil because there were no roads into this remote region. This isolation protected the rain forest and the Amazon Indians who had lived in the rain forest for centuries taking from the forest only what they needed to live. The few items that they needed from outside such as some articles of clothing, salt, and some medicines were brought to them by a trader in a special boat called a *regatão.* These items were exchanged for forest products.

The first non-Indian settlers came to the rain forest in the mid-1960s when the Brazilian government built the Belém-Brasília Highway connecting Belém at the mouth of the Amazon River to the new capital city of Brasília. The government wanted to develop this isolated area and bring factories into the rain forest thereby providing jobs for the large numbers of unemployed people. In order to encourage industry to locate in these remote areas, the government offered monetary incentives. Monetary means relating to money, and incentive is something that makes one try or work harder. Some of the monetary incentives the government offered included cash, low taxes, and loans at low interest rates. Large numbers of individuals also entered the area in hopes of obtaining land inexpensively. The government also offered monetary incentives to them so that settlers could purchase seeds, fertilizers, pesticides, and insecticides that they would need to start farms.

The hundreds of thousands of people who rushed to this area for jobs in manufacturing, farming, and ranching were only the beginning. As their numbers grew, additional secondary roads were needed and more forest areas were cleared. In the 1970s the government built still more major roads including the Transamazon Highway, a 3,100-mile (5,000-kilometer) east-west highway spanning the Amazon Basin at its widest point. The government built villages and cities along the highway and marked off farm plots of about 250 acres (101 hectares) each. It recruited settlers for the area and encouraged them to plant crops.

Unfortunately the resettlement hoped for along the Transamazon Highway was largely unsuccessful. In laying out the road little consideration was given to the fertility of the land around it. Much of the land was hilly and most of the soil was of very poor quality and not suited to growing crops. One of the crops the government encouraged planting was rice, which was not a wise choice for several reasons. In most places soil was not ideal for growing rice. Unless harvested within a very short time, it is eaten by birds. It requires lots of people and machines for harvesting, and it is difficult and expensive to get to major markets.

Many people who have settled in the forest area since the 1960s, however, are not involved in subsistence farming.

These people are trying to develop cash crops and cattle that can be taken out of the forest and sold. They clear large sections of forest by bringing in bulldozers and chain saws. The land and other natural resources of New World tropics are being utilized much more extensively than ever before. Valuable wood, plants, animals, and other products are being removed or destroyed so fast they cannot regrow or repopulate. Minerals are *nonrenewable* resources. This means that their supply cannot be replenished once it is used up. When mines have been dug, and the valuable supply of minerals that exists buried beneath the rain forest is taken out, there will be no more of them.

In 1968 another major road, the Cuiabá–Pôrto Velho Highway, called BR-364, about one thousand miles (1,600 kilometers) long, was built through the heart of southwestern Amazonia, which opened up the area known as Rondônia. It is about the size of Great Britain and is located in the western Amazon close to the Bolivian border. Until recently it was only sparsely populated by the Indian tribes who had lived there in isolation for thousands of years. However, with the construction of BR-364, thousands of people flocked to the area in search of inexpensive land and the government set up resettlement projects that included villages with gravel roads, schools, law enforcement offices, and health clinics. Additional smaller roads were built so that even more remote areas could be reached.

Farmers planted crops such as sugarcane, bananas, papayas, corn, root vegetables resembling potatoes, and cassava. The latter is a group of tropical plants whose thick root yields a nourishing starch. Perhaps you have eaten tapioca pudding or use tapioca to thicken a fruit pie. Tapioca is a grain or flake from the cassava root.

The resettlement program offered peasant farmers who were too poor to buy land elsewhere 247 acres (100 hectares) of land in this remote part of the Amazon. Homesteading laws required that, in order to claim the land, the settler had to show that he had made "improvements" on it. Slash-and-burn agriculture was considered an improvement and was responsible for the clearing of 460 square miles of rain forest in Rondônia in 1975. However, by 1985, eleven thousand square miles of rain forest in this region had been destroyed. The soils are not suitable for crops and the areas of cleared forest are so large that they cannot regrow to duplicate the original forest. Therefore, this kind of farming is no longer a sustainable use of the forest, but is destroying it.

Conflicts between newcomers and Indians are frequent and some observers compare the settling of the "new frontier" in Rondônia to the settling of the American West. Settlers trespass on Indian land and disregard their beliefs and traditions. Many disputes among people are settled illegally in drunken brawls or by gunfire. In developing the resettlement program, there was little concern on the part of the government for the well-being of the Indians. In Rondônia the number of native forest people dramatically dropped. Many died from the common cold, measles, flu, and other illnesses to which they had never been exposed before the arrival of the colonists, who in turn became ill with tropical diseases such as malaria and yellow fever.

Because of the growing problems in Rondônia, the government decided it should take action. In 1981 it improved and paved BR-364 as part of a larger project called Polonoroeste (Northwest Brazil Integrated Development Program). The project also involved the construction of settlement centers designed to provide for the thousands of settlers who had come to the region.

Thirty-five percent of the rain forest in Rondônia has been disturbed or destroyed by the hundreds of thousands of newcomers seeking a better life there. Where once the majestic canopy towered above the lush vegetation, millions of acres of wasteland now exist. In 1988 alone an area the size of the state of Michigan was burned to clear land for farming. Because colonists are not knowledgeable about the forest, wild fires rage out of control. The Amazon is literally going up in smoke! Visibility is sometimes so poor that distant airports

The main highway connecting Rondônia to the population centers of Brazil to the south is BR-364. It was paved in 1984 with a loan from the World Bank.

must be periodically closed. The pall of smoke hanging over the Amazon can be seen on images transmitted to earth by Landsat satellites.

These satellites, operated by the National Aeronautics and Space Administration (NASA), give an overview of what is happening to tropical ecosystems. They pass over all points of the earth's surface every sixteen days and transmit images to receiving stations in the United States and other countries. From the data in these space "pictures," scientists can monitor the fires and the extent of forest cover in the tropics. In this way they can accurately determine the amount of deforestation going on. Based on this information a growing number of scientists in Brazil are expressing alarm about deforestation, and in the 1990s the country will launch its own satellites to more closely monitor changes in the rain forest.

In Rondônia the forest is cleared by felling the large trees and burning the vegetation during the dry season. The resulting ash contains nutrients from the plants and temporarily improves the soil.

A large amount of the funding for Polonoroeste was made possible by the World Bank. It is a huge organization that was set up in 1945 to help rebuild Europe after World War II and to promote economic and social development of underdeveloped, or Third World, nations. The ownership of the World Bank is divided among 152 countries. The United States owns 18 percent and provides more money than any of the other countries. This contribution must be approved by the United States Congress. Because the United States has always had the largest share of votes, the president of the World Bank has been an American and the bank's headquarters are in Washington, D.C.

The World Bank and other international development banks make long-term loans to help improve living conditions and provide technical expertise to poor nations. This money is supplemented by money provided by the recipient country and from other loans. In the Polonoroeste Project, the World Bank loaned Brazil about $430 million to build roads and places for people to live. Though sometimes money lent by international development banks is spent on small projects, it is more often spent on large-scale projects such as irrigation for agriculture, dams for *hydroelectric* power plants to supply electricity for industries that can then locate in remote areas, and for roads built into the wilderness.

The World Bank has been criticized for not adequately considering the effects on the environment when deciding the merits of a loan and of not enforcing environmental safeguards once a project is underway. Belatedly in 1981 the World Bank required that areas of rain forest be set aside and conserved, but this policy was difficult to enforce. Several years later, however, the bank did suspend millions of dollars from the Polonoroeste project, citing environmental reasons.

The World Bank, Japan, Canada, the United States, and European nations are all partners with Brazil in the largest Amazonian development program undertaken to date. It is the Carajás Program, established to extract minerals from the earth. Deposits of high grade iron *ore* found in Pará along the Trombetas River are thought to be the largest in the world. An ore is the mineral that is mined to obtain a substance that it contains. Iron ore is mined for iron, used in making steel. This region also contains rich deposits of nickel, tin, gold, copper, and bauxite. Bauxite is the raw material that comes out of a clayey substance and is the principal ore in aluminum.

After the rain forest is cut down, mines are developed and the necessary roads and buildings are constructed. A railroad track was laid so that trains can transport the iron ore from the Carajás Mountains to Maraba for smelting, a process whereby the valuable material is taken out of the ore. Then

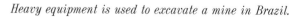

Heavy equipment is used to excavate a mine in Brazil.

it is taken to the Atlantic port of São Luís, where it is put into blast furnaces and processed into pig iron.

The heat in these furnaces is produced by burning charcoal, which is derived from burning *fuelwood.* This is the term used for wood cut from trees so that it can be burned as fuel. The logs you burn in your fireplace or wood-burning stove are fuelwood. (*Timber,* however, is wood that is made into something such as furniture, paper products, or houses.) So much charcoal is required that large areas of the forest are being chopped down. The wood is burned in earthen igloos to produce the charcoal that is sold to the iron industry.

Industrialization of the Amazon has created a huge demand for electricity. The rivers of the Amazon Basin contain an enormous capacity for generating hydroelectric power. A dam or wall is built across a river to hold back the water. Then the flow of water through turbines, engines whose central shaft is fitted with a series of blades that are turned by water moving against them, can be controlled. This motion turns the shaft of a generator to produce electricity, which is carried by wires to users.

Damming a river creates great changes in the river and the land around it. Behind the dam a *reservoir,* which is an artificial lake, is created, flooding the land and killing many plants and animals that lived there. Because the river is no longer free flowing, changes in the amount of oxygen in the water and in the temperature occur that can be harmful to fish. Also, some kinds of ocean fish that swim up rivers to lay their eggs cannot get beyond the dam to their spawning grounds. A dam prevents the normal rise and fall of the river and restricts the amount of water reaching the floodplains below it. As a result some species of plants and animals can no longer live in these wetlands.

When the Tucuruí Dam on the Tocantins River in the Amazon was completed in 1986, it was the fourth-largest dam in the world. It is twelve miles (nineteen kilometers) long and flooded 533,520 acres (216,000 hectares) of rain forest, home to thousands of animals and many Indian people of the forest. The Tucuruí Dam provides electric power to the Carajás iron ore project, the aluminum smelter and refinery near Belém, and other industries in northern Brazil. Many Brazilians believe the building of these immense hydroelectric projects is essential for progress and hope with more industries selling more products that they, too, will be able to afford to buy the material goods enjoyed by people in the developed world.

Destruction of the rain forest is occurring not only in an attempt by individual nations to meet their peoples' own needs but also as a response to demands from other countries. Construction of the Transamazon Highway made it possible for large equipment to be brought into the rain forest. In the final stages of clearing a rain forest, management and ownership of the land is often transferred from small farmers to large international corporations. Wealthy individuals and companies buy land inexpensively from settlers who can no longer farm it. Consequently, the settlers move deeper into the forest to find new areas to cut and burn.

Logging and cattle ranching are the two major activities causing destruction of the rain forest in Central and South America. Timber companies may hire migrant workers to do the dangerous work of felling the large trees with chain saws. New roads into the forest enable heavy diesel logging trucks to transport the giant logs to a sawmill. Loggers often cut only the most valuable hardwood and over 40 percent of the wood is wasted.

Most of the timber is sold to industrialized nations such as the United States. It is used to make pulp for paper and cardboard and in the construction of houses and boats and in the making of furniture. The United States is the largest importer of plywood in the world and almost half of it comes from rain forest trees. Try to determine what kind of wood the furniture in your house is made from. If it is oak, pine, or maple it probably came from trees in a temperate forest. If you have beds, bureaus, desks, tables, chairs, and even salad bowls made from teak, rosewood, mahogany, or tropical cedar, it came from the tropics. Most families have some of both temperate and tropical woods.

Conversion of rain forests to pasture for beef cattle also accounts for much of the destruction of New World tropics. After the trees have been cut and the land has been torched, grasses such as Australian grass are planted to make the land suitable for grazing. In Central America between 1950 and 1975, the amount of pasture that was created out of rain forest

Herd of beef cattle on land in Brazil that has been converted from tropical rain forest to pasture

doubled, as did the number of beef cattle. Nevertheless, after a few years the soil wears out and the cattle refuse to eat the weeds that grow in place of pasture grasses. Sometimes chemicals are used to kill the weeds and then fertilizer is applied to the soil in an attempt to return its fertility.

In the 1960s the United States began to import beef from Central America. Cattle raised there are grass fed and produce leaner beef than grain-fed cattle raised in America. Land in the tropics costs less and wages and benefits for workers are lower, which makes a larger profit for the owners of these cattle ranches. Beef from Central America comes to this country in refrigerated trucks and is sold to meat packers and brokers. It is sometimes mixed with United States beef and may eventually wind up in some luncheon meats, hot dogs, soups, and pet foods. At one time Central American beef was used in the hamburgers sold in some fast-food restaurants.

Almost all of Brazil's beef exports go to Western Europe. This is because United States laws forbid importation of fresh or frozen beef from that area because of a cattle disease that exists there. However, some Brazilian beef does come into our country in the form of canned products.

Ironically, when the rain forest is destroyed the land that once sustained an abundance of plants and animals can no longer support a pasture for cattle. The earth is no longer protected by the umbrellalike canopy, and the hot tropical sun shines on the ground where only dim sunlight shone before. Humidity drops, hot dry winds blow, and the thin sandy soil bakes in the heat and even shows cracks in places. With the canopy gone the earth is unprotected from driving rain. Rivulets of water form on the ground and carry the topsoil away. Within ten years the grasses decline and new pasture must be carved out of the rain forest.

In other areas forest is cut down for *plantations.* Plantations are farms or large estates where a group of plants, often of one kind, is planted, cared for, and sold. In the New World tropics many of the plantations have been established only since the 1960s. Sugarcane, bananas, pineapples, coffee,

Cutting sugarcane in Ecuador

cacao, and palm oil are some of the export crops, which means they are sold to foreign markets. Many plantations are owned by companies such as Coca-Cola, Borden, and Nestle, names familiar to most people in the industrialized world.

Many foods that we enjoy every day that are cultivated on plantations have their origin in New World rain forests. When coffee trees are about four years old they produce small berries, each of which contains two seeds, the coffee beans. Sugar cane, a member of the grass family, is also grown on plantations. The stalks grow to be twenty feet tall, and after being cut into pieces, the cane is crushed and further refined before appearing in its familiar forms on your table. Bananas, pineapples, and papayas are tropical American fruits. Nuts such as cashews, Brazil nuts, and peanuts are all native to the New World tropics. Even chicle, for many years the main ingredient in chewing gum, comes from a tropical tree.

However, the tropical food that may rate as number one among most people is chocolate. Although now a multibillion-dollar industry, the delights of eating chocolate, which comes from the seeds of the cacao tree, have been known for thousands of years. The Maya Indians of Central America and the Aztec Indians of Mexico planted cacao trees long before Columbus voyaged to America. Historians think that English importers probably made a spelling error, and that is why we use the word cocoa instead of cacao.

Cacao trees grow wild in tropical rain forests and are cultivated in the New World tropics on large plantations in Brazil and Ecuador. When grown on plantations or in orchards, cacao is usually planted along with rubber or banana trees to more closely resemble the shady environment of the rain forest. Cacao trees on plantations grow close together and if one tree becomes diseased or attacked by pests, other trees are often infected also. Insecticides are not very effective and can be harmful to the environment. They must be applied during the period of development that coincides with the rainy season and the rain rapidly washes the chemicals off the trees. Scientists are studying cacao trees that grow wild in the jungles of Brazil and Central America to see if more disease-resistant types of trees can be found.

Compared with many of the towering rain forest trees, the cacao tree is quite short, growing usually only to a height of twenty-five feet (7.6 meters). It is an evergreen with large oval

When the green pods of the cacao tree ripen they turn yellow.

shiny leaves. It takes four to five years from the time the tree is planted for it to bear fruit called pods.

Small waxy flowers, which can be white, pink, yellow, or bright red, grow directly on the trunk and the branches of the tree. These become the pods. The tree has an unusual appearance because the ten-inch-long, football-shaped pods are attached directly to its trunk and branches. Harvesters cut the pods from the trees and split them open horizontally with machetes. Each open pod with its rows of white seeds, called beans, resembles a mouthful of pulpy white teeth.

After the cacao beans are scooped out, they are put in piles and covered with banana leaves or palm fronds and are left to ferment. This causes the pulpy part around the seeds to rot, and dries out the beans. Fermenting takes away the bitter taste from the beans and brings out their flavor. Then the beans are shipped in sacks to other countries, where manufacturers roast and grind them before melting them into a gooey chocolate syrup that is the basis for all the chocolate we eat. If you cupped your hands together, you could hold about as many cacao beans as would be used in a sixteen-ounce candy bar.

Chocolate is not the only product we get from cacao trees. High pressure can be used to extract cocoa butter from the chocolate syrup. Although this is the basis for white chocolate, it is frequently used in suntan lotions, cosmetics, and soaps because of its oily smooth consistency.

In addition to food, tropical plants provide us with many nonedible products and medicines. Kapok is the silky fibers around the seeds of the kapok tree which are used as a filling for life preservers, pillows, and other things. Tropical resins and gums, the yellowish or brownish substances that come from the sap of some trees, are used in varnishes, glues, and plastics. Vegetable waxes, dyes, and oils are used as lubricants in machinery, and some chemicals in soap and lipstick come from rain forest plants. About one-quarter of all modern medicines are derived from tropical plants or are manufactured by pharmaceutical companies that copy the chemical blueprints of these tropical plants. They include curare, a medicine used as an anesthetic and to relax muscles, which comes from a tropical vine. Quinine, used to treat malaria, a mosquito-borne disease marked by periods of chills and fevers, comes from the bark of the cinchona tree.

Indians of the rain forest have used its plants for healing purposes for thousands of years. The medicine man of the tribe is called the "shaman" and knows how to use the resources of the forest to cure illness and disease. The bark of the fiddlewood tree that grows in Central America can be used in a herbal bath to cure the sores caused by a tropical parasite. Or if you had an earache, the shaman would find a particular kind of fungus, *Gloeporus thelephroides,* that grows in white clumps on rotting wood. He would then squeeze the juice from the fungus and drip it through a curled leaf into your ear. If you also had a cold and cough he might make some tea for you from *Renealmia,* a plant with red fruit.

Today scientists called *ethnobotanists* study the ancient ways tribal people use rain forest plants for healing. They greatly respect the shaman's knowledge. Under the guidance of the shaman the ethnobotanist collects plants that are believed to contain medicinal properties. These are sent to modern research laboratories for analysis and testing. The

National Cancer Institute is spending millions of dollars to collect samples of rain forest plants, and a number of these appear to be promising in the treatment of cancer, AIDS, arthritis, and other diseases. As destruction of the rain forest continues, some scientists worry that lifesaving plant species may become extinct before their value is even known to modern people.

Just as tropical medicines are vital to our health, natural rubber is an essential part of the way we live. Radial tires on cars must be made partially from natural rubber in order to have the proper elasticity for a smooth ride and to be able to withstand heat that is produced when the brakes are applied. The rest of the rubber in tires is of a *synthetic* rubber, produced from petroleum.

For almost fifty years beginning around 1870, Manaus, the capital of the state of Amazonia, was the rubber capital of the world. Located one thousand miles (1,600 kilometers) inland from the Atlantic coast where the black Negro River and the muddy Solimôes River combine with other smaller rivers to form the mighty Amazon, Manaus is a city carved out of the jungle. During its rubber-producing years, thousands of men came upriver by canoe every week to gather latex, the milky sap of the rubber tree. People made huge fortunes by selling rubber to other countries. Manaus became a wealthy city with fashionable mansions, a grand hotel, a town square complete with a Swiss clock, and even an elegant opera house.

In the early 1900s rubber plantations were established by the British in their Asian colonies. By about 1910 plantation-grown rubber became so available that it caused the price to drop significantly. Later, in the 1940s, synthetic rubber was developed and Manaus went into decline. In the early 1960s the Brazilian government offered monetary incentives to encourage growth and development in Manaus. Now many people there are employed in jobs that have been created as a result of government monetary incentives.

The United States uses more than one-quarter of the world's supply of natural rubber. Tires for bulldozers, aircraft, and even space shuttles are made almost entirely of natural rubber. It is also used in products as diverse as boots and gloves, hoses, bicycle tires, sneakers and running shoes, hot-water bottles, and pet toys. If you buy a squeaky toy for your dog or cat the label probably says 100 PERCENT LATEX.

Latex is used to make natural rubber. It comes from the rubber tree, *Hevea brasiliensis,* which grows wild in the South American rain forest. For centuries Indians used latex to waterproof things before modern people used it in the manufacture of rubber. There might be about six hundred wild rubber trees in one thousand acres of rain forest. Because these trees are widely scattered in the forest, they are more resistant to disease. However, when they are planted close together in rows on rubber plantations, they are susceptible to a fungus, the South American leaf blight. This weakens and may eventually kill the trees. Therefore, rubber plantations are more established in the Old World tropics, where this fungus does not thrive. However, even these rubber trees were started with seeds of the Amazonian species. Whether growing wild or in plantations, rubber trees must be about five years old before they produce latex.

The latex is processed in various ways. Some plantations have processing plants that make crude rubber from the latex. Water and an acid are added to the latex, causing it to form solid particles. The rubber pieces separate from the liquid and rise to the surface. Then they are put through rollers that form them into sheets of rubber. Sometimes latex is sent in liquid form from plantations to processing plants. When this method is used, a preservative is added to the latex so that it will not harden. The oldest method of making crude rubber is by drying latex over a smoky fire. Long, broad wooden paddles are dipped in the latex and slowly turned in the smoke. As the latex congeals, it begins to form a thin layer of rubber. When it is thick enough, it is removed from the paddles and formed into balls.

Latex is collected from rubber trees by rubber tappers called "seringueiros." At dawn they hack their way through the jungle underbrush in search of rubber trees. In one day a seringueiro may tap between three hundred and five hundred trees, and for this work he earns about $1,200 a year. With a sharp machete, he makes a series of angled cuts halfway around the diameter of the tree. At the lowest point of the cuts, the rubber tapper hangs a tin cup.

Slowly the latex oozes from the tree's bark and trickles down into the cup. Just as tapping a maple tree for sap does not harm it, tapping rubber trees for latex causes no damage to the tree. After tapping a number of trees, the seringueiro returns to each tree to collect the latex. Less than a measuring cup is collected from each tree.

In Acre, a neighboring state of Rondônia, thousands and thousands of rubber tappers will lose their livelihood if the forest is destroyed. With overcrowding in Rondônia, the Inter-American Development Bank, also funded mostly from the United States, is loaning $147 million to pave a dirt highway into Acre. This road will connect the cities of Porto Velho and Rio Rianco and penetrate deeper into the Amazon forest. Loggers are clear-cutting the forest near the highway to harvest the timber and prepare the land for farming and cattle ranching.

When the seringueiros opposed the cutting down of the forest, the owners of some cattle ranches hired gunmen to intimidate and even harm them. And on December 22, 1988, Chico Mendes, a Brazilian who had been a seringueiro since the age of nine, was killed because of his brave efforts to preserve the rain forest. Francisco Mendes, or Chico as he was called, was born in 1944 in the rain forest. He was the son of a seringueiro and he had little formal education. He lived with his wife and children in a hut. Nearby he maintained a garden and a couple of livestock.

In the mid-1970s he and other seringueiros became concerned about the dwindling number of rubber trees and the large areas of rain forest that were being cut down and reduced to wasteland. Chico became the seringueiros' leader and proposed that areas of the rain forest be protected. This would not only maintain parts of the forest for rubber tapping, but also would provide a sanctuary for rain forest plants, animals, and people. There were times when whole families of protesters sat in the path of bulldozers attempting to clear land for cattle ranches. They were so courageous in their fight against the destruction of the rain forest that Chico became known internationally for his often successful efforts to save the tropical forest. He was presented with numerous awards including one from the United Nations Environment

Programme. Because he was a champion of saving the rain forest, Chico became the enemy of those who wanted to develop it. During the last year of his life he lived under constant threats of death. He said if he were killed he wanted no flowers at his funeral because they would be taken from the rain forest.

In spite of the fact that Chico was given police protection, he was shot on December 22, 1988, as he stepped from his small hut into his backyard. Chico's death was reported in newspapers and on television around the world. In spite of assassins' bullets, Chico's ideas would not die. In Washington, D.C., the Environmental Defense Fund created the Chico Mendes Fund to carry on his work. Chico's death made his followers determined that he had not died in vain and they continue to protest the development of the rain forest.

4
Rescuing the Tropical Rain Forest

Much like the lifeguard at the beach whose knowledge, skills, and courage save a swimmer from drowning, so must each of us recognize that the rain forests are in danger and take the plunge to rescue them. For both the swimmer and the rain forests there is little time to spare. Like the watchful lifeguard, we need to be aware that the rain forests are in trouble and heed their urgent cries for help. If people who live in the temperate as well as the tropical zones do not begin to think of themselves as protectors of the New World tropics, predictions that within sixty years these forests will be destroyed may come true. If this is allowed to happen between one-third and one-half of all species living today will become extinct.

The loss of many tropical species greatly affects *biodiver-*

sity. Biological means relating to biology, the study of plants and animals and how they live. *Diversity* is the condition of being different or in a variety of forms. When the two words *biological* and *diversity* are combined into one, *biodiversity,* it means the variety of living things. Rain forests are extremely rich in biodiversity. One naturalist, for example, reported forty-three species of ants in a single Peruvian tree. How many examples of biodiversity can you find where you live? Depending on where you live, the possibilities are people, a dog, a cow, a gerbil, an ant, a tree, a housefly, beans and carrots in your garden, a robin, an African violet plant, a snake, and many more. Each living thing is unlike the other and the whole group is an example of biodiversity.

What value should we place on biodiversity? Many people value species according to their worth to human beings. The cow is important because she gives milk, the beans and carrots are rich in vitamins, and the tree could be cut down and used to build a house. The African violet adds beauty to a room in your house, the sight of the robin in your yard gives you pleasure, and the gerbil is a pet you enjoy. But what about the ant? While many people given the opportunity would happily eliminate this species, others would argue that all living things have a right to exist and would recognize its place in the ecosystem.

People sometimes become more interested in protecting individual species of animals that may be endangered than in preserving the animals' habitats, which are so necessary for their survival. For example, we are ardent about saving the whales but don't give much thought to the well-being of the oceans. While some people are attempting to save the Amazon manatee (sea cow), which has become an endangered species because of overhunting for its meat, oil, and hide, logging and mining operations continue to pollute the waterways in which these animals live. Millions of plants are coming closer and closer to extinction, and yet they don't arouse our passion as much as endangered animals even though plants produce food, medicine, fibers, and products used in industry upon which we depend for our comfort and survival.

Living things have such complex relationships in the tropics that even valiant efforts to save a particular species may not ensure survival if the habitat is destroyed. An example of this is the Brazil nut tree, which grows in the South American rain forest. While not an endangered species, it is dependent upon its environment for survival. You may be familiar with the Brazil nut, the three-sided nut you may have eaten or seen for sale in your supermarket. Flowers of the Brazil nut tree are pollinated by large bees and form a round or pear-shaped fruit. Each fruit is about three to four times the size of a baseball and has an extremely hard outer layer. Inside the fruit, the nuts or seeds grow in circular layers.

Without the help of the agouti (a large rodent) and the bearded saki (a kind of monkey), the fruits of the Brazil nut tree might lie on the ground for years. However, both of these animals have teeth that are sharp enough to crack open the hard fruit containing the nuts. The agouti, by burying the nuts in various places, some of which the animal does not dig up and eat, scatters the seeds throughout the forest. The bearded saki drops some of the seeds as it eats. But at the sound of the chain saw or the crackle of fire the animals flee to an undisturbed part of the forest. Even if the Brazil nut tree were spared, it could not reproduce in the forest without the help of bees and animals.

Extinction is a natural process. Estimates of the number of species that have ever lived since the time life first appeared on earth are in the hundreds of millions. Today it is thought that between five million and thirty million species are alive in the world and of these most are insects. The reasons why species become extinct are not well understood. Changes in climate such as those that resulted from the Ice Ages, an imbalance between the number of predators and prey, and the impact of a meteor hitting the earth and creating so much dust in the atmosphere it blocked out the sunlight and interfered with the growth of plants are some of the theories that try to explain extinction.

The present rate of extinction is abnormally high. Some biologists think that in the tropics the rate of extinction might become thousands of times greater than is natural. The World Resources Institute, a Washington, D.C.–based environmental research organization, warns that a hundred species a day may disappear in the coming decades! Since so many plants and animals in the New World tropics have never been collected, identified, and studied we may not even know with any certainty how many are being lost.

Because we live in the Northern Hemisphere the New World tropics seem very far away. In addition, our modern life-styles often separate us from the natural world. Yet we are just as dependent on the earth's ecosystems as Indian forest dwellers whose primitive ways of providing food, clothing, and shelter have changed little in over ten thousand years.

Whether human beings drink from a factory-made glass or from the dried hollow shell of the fruit of the calabash tree, as some Indians do, we need adequate supplies of clean water to drink. Unlike the native forest dweller who takes water directly from the ground or a local stream, when we turn on the faucet or buy bottled water in the supermarket we do not see where it comes from. It is easy to lose our sense of linkage to the natural world. The water we drink, the air we breathe, and the oceans we swim in are all part of the global environment shared by people everywhere.

Tropical rain forests are important in the regulation of climate in areas in which they exist as well as in distant lands. If extensive areas of New World tropics are destroyed, changes in the forest land itself bring about changes in the climate. The protective canopy that filtered sunlight and absorbed the force of driving rains will be gone. The water, which normally slowly soaks into the the spongelike root network of the forest, will rush into local streams and rivers, bringing much of the soil with it. During rainy seasons this will cause increased *erosion* and flooding. Conversely, during the dry season, there will be no stored water in the roots of trees or in shaded forest ponds. The sun will bake and dry out the soil. Some experts believe the area could even turn into a "dust bowl." The land on which a rich green tropical forest once stood enveloped in a gentle mist will eventually resemble a desert.

You are probably asking: "How can rain forests influence the weather in the Temperate Zone?" When the forest is cut or burned down, the leaves necessary for *transpiration* die. Transpiration is the process by which green leaves give off water vapor through tiny openings called *stomata* on their outer layer.

In a *terrarium,* a closed container enclosing a garden of small plants, you can easily observe the effects of transpiration. The plants use the moisture from the soil to live, releasing some of it through their leaves as transpiration occurs. Moisture condenses on the sides of the terrarium. These drops fall to the bottom of the container, keeping the soil moist.

Another way you can see the effect of transpiration is by wrapping a clear plastic bag around a plant and securing it tightly around the base of the plant where it enters the soil. Within a day or two you will see droplets of moisture forming on the inside of the plastic. This moisture has been given off by the plant through transpiration.

In the rain forest, moisture from transpiration joins with that which evaporates from surface water in the forest. About one-fifth of the fresh water that is found on the earth's surface in rivers, lakes, and streams is in Amazonia. The water that

Destruction of the rain forest makes the land more subject to erosion.

evaporates from these sources and transpires from foliage eventually forms the clouds that produce the rain in the tropical forest.

In addition to changing the amount of rainfall, the destruction of the tropical rain forests can also cause changes in temperature. Like trees and plants all over the world, those in the rain forest remove carbon dioxide from the air as photosynthesis occurs. Carbon dioxide is a colorless, odorless gas composed of carbon and oxygen. When you open a can of cola, it is the carbon dioxide in the soda that makes the fizz. People and animals put carbon dioxide into the air when they breathe out. Plants take in carbon dioxide and give off oxygen. The plants in the tropical rain forests are one of the world's greatest sources of oxygen.

Since the dawn of the Industrial Revolution in the mid-nineteenth century, the amount of carbon dioxide in the atmosphere has been steadily increasing. The reasons for this are twofold. First, fossil fuels (coal, oil, and natural gas) have been burned in much greater quantity to provide power for heavy machinery, to fuel internal combustion engines in cars and other vehicles, and to heat buildings and houses. As they burn, these fuels release carbon dioxide into the atmosphere. The second reason is the burning of the tropical rain forest. This increases the carbon dioxide in the atmosphere not only because it is released as the trees burn, but also because the trees are no longer removing it from the atmosphere as photosynthesis occurs.

The earth's atmosphere, which naturally contains small amounts of carbon dioxide, has always served as a "blanket" for our planet. Sunlight enters the atmosphere and warms the earth's surface and the oceans. Heat from the ground and seas is trapped or absorbed by the lower atmosphere, which acts like a barrier. Scientists believe that increased amounts of carbon dioxide cause more of the earth's heat to be retained by the atmosphere than in the past. This is called the "greenhouse effect."

During the past century the global temperature has risen by one degree centigrade (1.8 degrees F). If this trend continues, scientists think our lives could change considerably. Increased warming on a global scale may shift rainfall patterns in the Northern Hemisphere in such a way as to decrease rainfall in the American Midwest. Temperatures may no longer be suitable for crops that have grown in certain areas for hundreds of years. There may also be stronger hurricanes along our coasts, and polar ice caps may melt. Vast amounts of the earth's water is frozen into huge ice masses at the North and South poles. Even a slight temperature increase will cause large quantities of ice to melt, resulting in rising sea levels all over the world. Low-lying areas including major coastal cities such as New York, Los Angeles, and New Orleans could be flooded.

Although destroying the rain forests can have potentially severe effects on climate and biodiversity, industrialized nations cannot deny others their right to develop their own natural resources. This would be akin to a country in Central or South America saying to the United States 150 years ago that pioneers, cowboys, prospectors, and others who were seeking a better way of life or a fast fortune could not go west. Perhaps through hard lessons learned through development of our own frontier we can help Third World nations to avoid our mistakes.

When the American West was settled there was no plan to protect the environment. Native Americans had used the West's natural resources in a sustainable way for thousands of years. However, within a few short decades of the opening up of the West, the vast herds of buffalo had disappeared and bloody conflicts arose between Indians and settlers. The building of roads became a symbol of progress, and there was little concern about the effect of development on native Indian tribes and on the plants and animals that inhabited these lands.

Some might wish that all of the remaining New World rain forests would be preserved in their original condition. But realistically the treasures of the tropics are not going to be left untouched. The huge increases in the human population that are occurring in the tropical countries make the use and occupation of these lands almost certain. Experts predict that there will be increasing poverty and starvation if we do not figure out how to make massive increases in our food production. The question then becomes: How can we preserve the rain forests and have enough land and food for the growing populations of the undeveloped world? The solution undoubtedly lies in finding a balance between utilization and preservation of the rain forests. Then much of the destruction that has accompanied past development can be avoided.

In the New World tropics there is a growing appreciation of the uniqueness of tropical rain forests and with this is coming a sincere desire to conserve them. Reserves and national parks are patches of land that have been left in their natural state. In reserves the land is completely untouched so it can be used for scientific study and education. If land is designated as a national park it may have limited development and may be used by tourists for outdoor recreation such as hiking and canoeing.

Critical questions when establishing these "park islands" are how large they have to be in order to protect species of plants and animals that live within them and which areas are most important to save. The larger the park the more species will survive. Mammals and birds need larger areas of intact rain forests than insects, spiders, and lower animals. Even a 100,000-hectare (247,000-acre) wildlife preserve may not provide enough prey to keep a population of jaguars in good health. A buffer zone around the park is necessary to insulate it from human activities outside its borders.

While some parts of tropical rain forests are left undeveloped, other parts may be used on a limited basis, leaving some of the land in its natural state. Before any of the rain forest is cut, an inventory of the creatures that live there should be taken. Scientists should take leaf and flower samples for the identification of trees and plants. Animal species should be accounted for. Using rotting fruit as bait, butterflies will fly into nets. Mammals are caught in traps and birds become entangled in almost invisible nets. Insects are attracted to light and reptiles can be caught at night in a variety of ways. After the rain forests are cut and torched a second census is taken. One of the things that has been learned is that "wildlife corridors," which are strips of forests leading from cleared to undisturbed areas, can increase the number of animals that survive.

National parks have been created in Amazonia and Central America. The first national park in Amazonia was established in 1974. Since that time Brazil has established two giant parks, the Amazonas National Park and the Rio Negro National Park. These, together with smaller parks such as Brazil's Tapajos National Park and Peru's Canaima National Park and Manu National Park, comprise a considerable amount of land in Amazonia, but it is not nearly enough. Assuming that development continues at its present rate, more than half of the species that live in Amazonia will become extinct during our lifetime unless additional huge parks and reserves are created soon. In Central America there are forty-six national parks. Three-fourths of these have been established since 1970. Costa Rica in particular is making remarkable efforts to save its forests.

Third World nations, so rich in biodiversity, have so little in accumulated wealth. Setting land aside to protect the envi-

Native hut in a cleared patch of the forest

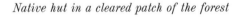

ronment is a luxury that many countries find difficult to afford. In their desire to provide adequate food and a higher standard of living for their people, many Third World nations in the tropics have tried unsuccessfully to adopt the modern farming methods that have been so effective in the Temperate Zone. These include clearing the land and planting a single crop, using large equipment that runs on gasoline rather than having animals do the work, and applying chemicals to the soil to keep it fertile and to plants to keep them free of weeds and insect pests. For a number of reasons when these techniques are transferred to the New World tropics they often do not work very well.

In addition to differences in climate, the soil in the tropics is very thin and easily carried away by the frequent harsh rains. This erosion causes the loss of nutrients. When equipment breaks down, the parts and expertise needed to repair it may not be available. Profits are eaten up by the huge investments that are necessary in order to keep the farm operating. When a single crop is planted, it is more susceptible to disease. Chemicals are expensive and require knowledge of modern farming methods in order to be applied correctly so as not to endanger the health of workers or other living things.

Large scale modern farming methods are not suited to tropical land. Therefore, new methods need to be found to sustain rain forest areas. *Agroforestry* combines the knowledge of Indian forest dwellers who know how to use the rain forest with the knowledge of modern technology and science. Rather than raising a single crop, the farmer raises a blend of crops, animals, and trees in a way that is in harmony with the natural environment. Instead of bulldozing entire sections of forest for planting, some large trees are left standing. Then the farmer plants such traditional crops as maize, cassava, sweet potatoes, and beans among the trees.

The trees may provide fruits and nuts as well as some animal habitat while at the same time preventing erosion. The fallen leaves and pods from the trees are either fed to animals as fodder or plowed into the soil as fertilizer. In another method, strips of the forest remain undisturbed while rows of valuable species of trees such as bananas, cacao, and coffee are planted in alternating rows. Planted trees benefit from leaf litter, are more disease resistant, and lessen erosion.

In Latin America a program to save the green or common iguana is an example of an agroforestry project meeting with success. Twenty years ago these large lizards were so plentiful in rain forests from Mexico to Brazil that they were sold for food in great numbers in open-air markets. However, in recent years because of habitat destruction and overhunting the number of iguanas has sharply declined.

The green iguana is greenish brown in color and can grow to a length of six feet, although about half of its length is tail. Along the middle of the back the iguana has a ridge of scales that makes it resemble reptiles that lived during prehistoric times. Although the thought of eating lizard for dinner may not appeal to you, the green iguana has been a sought-after source of protein in the New World tropics for thousands of years. There it is nicknamed the "chicken of the trees." The iguana is cooked in a pot of boiling water and its meat can be made into a spicy stew.

In the wild, iguanas clamber up into the canopy. They like

to spend lazy days sunbathing in the treetops, where there is plenty of leafy vegetation for them to eat. They are cold-blooded animals and do not have any built-in control over their body temperature as mammals do. Warming their bodies in the sun speeds up digestion of their vegetarian meals. Native forest dwellers hunt the iguana using slingshots and traps or by shaking the branches on which the iguana naps so that it drops to the ground and can be captured.

Like other reptiles, the green iguana lays eggs. Females deposit their leathery eggs in underground burrows at a

The iguana is a large plant-eating tropical American lizard that has a ridge of tall scales along the middle of the back.

depth that provides the ideal temperature for hatching. Usually only about half of the eggs produce young, and of these roughly 5 percent survive their first year. The rest fall prey to snakes, opossums, and other animals.

In 1983 the Smithsonian Tropical Research Institute began the Iguana Management Project in Panama. The goal was to learn how to raise iguanas in captivity so they could continue to be an important source of food for local people. It was hoped that this knowledge would help to rebuild the population of iguanas in the wild. Biologists collected several dozen female iguanas and put them in a dirt pen. Within the enclosure, they buried clay pipe tunnels which led to cement block chambers. The iguanas deposited their fertilized eggs in these underground "nests." The researchers dug up the eggs and kept them at the right temperature using heat lamps. When the finger-length iguanas hatched, they were weighed, measured, and fed a diet of fruit, flowers, and leaves. Because they were protected from predators, many more of them survived in captivity and gained weight faster that those that live in the wild.

When the iguanas are between seven months and one year old, they are distributed to farmers in Central American countries as part of the repopulation program. Farmers are taught how to create "shelter belts" between their land and the forest. Iguanas seek out these sunlit forest edges where, as in the canopy, they are able to bask in the sun and keep warm. When the iguanas are ready to reproduce, farmers help to ensure the survival of the eggs by building artificial tunnels composed of buried clay pipes leading to small concrete block enclosures that serve as nests. Iguana "ranches" can potentially supply more meat per acre than cattle ranches and remain productive for a much longer time. Iguana ranching is an example of a sustainable use of the rain forest because the resources of the forest are used without being destroyed.[5]

Many people in the richer developed nations are beginning to realize that their help is urgently needed if the precious heritage of the tropical rain forests is to be saved. Large moneylenders and governments must become more aware that intensive development such as mines, power plants, pulp mills, and other industries should be sited in locations that will have the least serious impact on the environment. When study and planning come before development, rather than letting it occur willy-nilly, the adverse effects can be softened.

Also, industrialized nations could compensate Third World nations for setting aside land to establish national parks and reserves. Compensation is something that makes up for something else. If you are baby-sitting and the parents are delayed arriving home they may pay you more than your hourly rate to compensate for the fact you had to stay longer than expected with their child. Industrialized nations could make up for the income the undeveloped country would derive from selling the timber, minerals, plants, and other rain forest products.

"Debt for nature" swaps are one way this can be done. These are complicated financial arrangements between conservation groups in the developed world that pay a portion of

5. Information about the Iguana Management Project was gathered from numerous reports describing the work of Dr. Dagmar Werner, a research scientist with the Smithsonian Tropical Research Institute in Panama.

In a few hours using powerful equipment such as this bulldozer, people can destroy tropical rain forests that have existed for millions of years.

the money Third World countries owe to banks. In exchange for helping to pay off the nation's debt, the groups obtain some voice in how the land should be used. Oftentimes they become involved in setting up environmental protection programs or in helping to set aside and protect lands for conservation.

The kind of actions that responsible governments, industries, and international agencies can make is spelled out in the *World Conservation Strategy* released in 1980. The United Nations Environment Programme, the International Union for Conservation of Nature and Natural Resources, and the World Wildlife Fund worked together to produce this important document. The strategy states that conservation and development must go hand in hand. Conservation programs that ignore development and people's needs will not have public acceptance. Only the kind of development that can be maintained for a long time and that enables people to make a living without destroying forests, pastures, and farmland or polluting water supplies should be allowed.

Americans and citizens of other industrialized countries consume more than their share of natural resources compared with people in less developed nations. People in the United States are also the largest consumers of wildlife in the world. When we purchase things, we often do not question what they are made of, or where they came from. Many rain forest animals are killed to satisfy people's desire for luxuries: fur of mammals, live birds, and patterned skin of snakes, lizards, caimans, and other reptiles.

When travelers buy wildlife products as souvenirs in foreign markets, they are often surprised to find that they are not allowed to keep them when entering the United States and in some instances must pay a large fine. This is because laws and international treaties have been enacted to protect threatened and endangered species.

Inspectors of the United States Fish and Wildlife Service and the United States Customs Service enforce laws passed to protect wild plants and animals. The Endangered Species Act prohibits all endangered and most threatened species from being imported or exported. The Convention on International Trade in Endangered Species in Wild Fauna and Flora (CITIES) is an international treaty signed by over one hundred nations. It regulates trade of plant and animal species that are threatened or endangered in certain countries. For example, most crocodile, lizard, and snakeskin products originating in Central and South American countries are prohibited from being brought into the United States without legal documentation approved by CITIES.

A United States Fish and Wildlife Service law enforcement officer says, "The beautiful fur of spotted cats is often tailored into fur coats. The jaguar, one of the largest and most elusive cats, is now an endangered species. Its populations have severely decreased because of hunting and forest destruction. There are four other species of spotted cats from the rain forests also used in international trade: the ocelot, Geoffroy's cat, little spotted cat, and the margay. Because these cats are so small, it may take nearly twenty-five pelts to produce a fur coat.

A United States Fish and Wildlife inspector exhibits some illegally imported wildlife products that originated in the New World Tropical Rain Forests. These include the furs of spotted cats, as well as crocodile, lizard, and snakeskin products.

"Many other protected species are also smuggled out of the New World tropics and into the United States. Live birds have been found hidden in suitcases, hair curlers, and even underneath cars. Young parrots are often stolen from their nest and smuggled across international borders. Some officials estimate nearly 150,000 birds are smuggled across the Mexican border each year. Most of these birds will die of stress before they arrive at the pet shops. The United States is the world's largest importer of parrots. Since many rain forest birds have become endangered, some Latin American countries now prohibit any live bird from being taken from their country.

"The New World rain forest supplies the international market with millions of live reptiles and reptile skins. The skins of the spectacled caiman and tegu lizard are commonly manufactured into handbags, belts, watchbands, and shoes. Many endangered reptiles are nearing extinction due to such a high demand for their skin. You may see live reptiles in your local pet shop. Many iguanas, lizards, boa constrictors, and freshwater turtles originating in the rain forests are smuggled into the United States to be sold as pets. In some states, it is illegal to own certain live reptiles since they can be dangerous."[6]

If you have a home freshwater aquarium, you may have species of tropical fish that are native to rivers and streams in the New World tropical rain forests. While almost all of these enter the United States legally, you may be interested in inquiring before you buy a particular species whether it has been bred in captivity or captured in the wild. Many

6. Quoted with permission of Public Affairs Office, Fish and Wildlife Service, Division of Law Enforcement, United States Department of Interior.

tetras, including the neon and cardinal tetras, as well as most catfish, are caught in the wild. However, most discuses, platy, angelfish, and guppies are raised on fish farms, such as those in Florida.

People in the developed world have a responsibility not to provide a ready market for living treasures of the rain forest. In so providing, they are severely affecting biodiversity in the tropics. The rare orchid in a bouquet or corsage, a coat made of the beautiful fur of spotted cats such as the ocelot, large snake and crocodile skins displayed on a wall, and colorful tropical birds caged in a pet store are indications that we must balance our own desire for something different and unusual with the needs of the animals.

You can help to educate others about the destruction of the New World tropics. One fun way of showing our tropical connections might be to plan a party which features a menu of tropical foods. Or perhaps your class can visit an aquarium, or a zoological or botanical garden, that has tropical species. Organize a fund-raising event such as a car wash to raise money to donate to conservation groups that have active programs dealing with the protection of habitats in the New World tropics. These include the World Wildlife Fund, the Environmental Defense Fund, the New York Zoological Society, and the Programme for Belize.

Belize is a small Central American nation about the size of New Hampshire. Unlike rain forest areas in some other countries, almost 70 percent of those in Belize are undisturbed. Over five hundred species of tropical birds, mammals including howler monkeys, tapirs, pumas, anteaters, manatees, and

Farmers in Third World countries often use animals to transport their produce to market.

jaguars, reptiles such as the poisonous fer-de-lance snake and the rare Morelet's crocodile, as well as huge numbers of spiders, worms, and insects live in Belizean rain forests. In parts of Belize where deforestation has occurred, land was converted to cattle ranches, banana and sugarcane plantations, and citrus groves.

Such projects awakened people in Belize to the threat posed by foreign investors. Searching for a way to improve the standard of living and at the same time protect natural resources, government officials sought the advice and help of organizations in Europe and the United States. The conservation program that developed as a result is called the Programme for Belize.

The goal of the Programme for Belize is to establish a 282,000-acre (114,170-hectare) reserve to be known as the Rio Bravo Conservation and Management Area. Scientists working at a research station within the reserve are studying ways the natural resources of the rain forest can be used without harming it. This includes wildlife tourism, agroforestry, and perhaps selected lumbering. Coca-Cola Foods has donated 42,000 acres (103,740 hectares) of land to the program and another 130,000 acres (321,100 hectares) will remain privately owned but managed in a way that supports conservation. Supporters of the program help to raise money to buy the remaining 110,000 acres (271,700 hectares). For every fifty dollars donated, one acre of land is added to the Rio Bravo conservation area. To date more than ninety schools in the United States have contributed to the Programme for Belize by raising money from activities such as bake sales and the collection of returnable bottles. If you

The lovely orchid, as well as the crocodile, are parts of the biodiversity that make up the tropical rain forest.

would like more information about this, write to the Programme for Belize.

For a fee you can become a member of the Rainforest Action Network, which has publications just for students. This organization will send you a monthly newsletter, tell you how to start a rain forest club at your school, refer you to places with information about recycling if your community does not already have such a program, and even help you find a pen pal in the New World tropics.

Perhaps you will become a leader in saving the tropics by deciding to pursue an advanced education in economics of the Third World, wildlife management, or tropical forest biology. Maybe you will be one of the brave scientists who study life high up in the canopy. Adapting modern rock-climbing techniques, these biologists ascend the towering trees of the rain forest. There they build a platform, part of which may have a tarp roof to keep a simple bed and supplies dry. Then they build a network of rope catwalks and bridges radiating out from the platform. This arrangement makes it possible for them to spend several days studying the canopy without coming down to the ground. Like the depths of the ocean, the heights of the canopy are almost unexplored.

With chain saws, bulldozers, and other powerful equipment, we can bring the giant trees of the rain forest, the very symbol of strength and majesty, crashing to the ground from their lofty heights in just a few hours. The effects of destroying tropical rain forests are becoming all too clear. Increasing numbers of plants and animals are tottering on the brink of extinction. Whether we live in developed or undeveloped parts of the world, cook our food over a wood fire or in a microwave oven, we are all members of the global community. If we get involved and do our part, we can save the rich tapestry of life which is the rain forest. In so doing, we are preserving a natural heritage that is millions of years old. By protecting the habitat of the fragile orchid and the mighty jaguar, we are safeguarding our own survival as well.

GLOSSARY

Aerial—Living or growing in the air rather than on the ground or in water.

Agroforestry—A method of farming that combines the knowledge of Indian forest dwellers with modern technology and science.

Algae—Simple plants usually living in water that do not have roots or flowers.

Amphibians—Organisms that are able to live on land or in water.

Bacteria—One-celled organisms that live in soil, water, air, or living things and are so tiny they can only be seen with a microscope.

Biodiversity—The variety of living things.

Biologists—Scientists who study living things.

Blowguns—Tubes of bamboo or reed through which poisonous darts are blown.

Bromeliads—Tropical plants of the pineapple family that grow on the trunks and branches of rain forest trees. They have thick, waxy leaves arranged in a circular cluster that form a tank that catches and stores water.

Bred—Reproduced or increased through sexual mating.

Camouflage—A disguise or false appearance that is used to hide something.

Canopy—The topmost layer of closely spaced spreading leaves and branches of tall trees.

Carnivorous—Feeding on animals.

Commensal—A relationship between two kinds of organisms in which one benefits and the other is neither benefited nor harmed.

Competition—A struggle between individuals of the same or different species for food, living space, mates, or other limited resources.

Conservation—The careful protection and preservation of natural resources.

Crowns—The leaves and upper branches of trees, which often form an umbrella shape in the rain forest.
Cultivate—To prepare and use land for growing crops.
Decomposers—Bacteria and fungi that break down dead plants and animals and return their nutrients to the soil.
Ecology—The study of the relationships of living things to one another and to their environment.
Emergents—The tallest trees in the tropical rain forest whose tops poke through above the canopy.
Endangered species—One in which the number of individuals is so low that it is in danger of becoming extinct.
Environment—The air, land, water, and all the living and nonliving things that make up a certain place.
Epiphytes—Plants such as aerial orchids, bromeliads, and many ferns and mosses that are supported by another plant but do not harm it.
Erosion—A slow wearing, washing, or eating away by the action of wind, water, or glacial ice.
Ethnobotanists—Scientists who study the ancient ways tribal people use tropical plants for healing.
Extinct—No longer existing, no longer active.
Fertilization—The union of male and female sex cells to form a new individual.
Fuelwood—Wood that is burned to produce heat.
Fungi—A group of plants that, like bacteria, cannot make their own food. Fungi include yeast, molds, and mushrooms. They aid in the decay of dead plants and animals.
Gap—An opening in the forest where sunlight can penetrate the forest floor.
Habitat—The place where a plant or an animal naturally lives and grows.
Hemisphere—One of the halves of the globe or earth.
Herbivorous—Feeding on plants.
Humus—Loamy, dark soil rich in nutrients.

Hydroelectric—Producing or having to do with the production of electricity by waterpower.
Insecticide—A chemical used to kill insects.
Lianas—Climbing vines that root in the ground but climb up into the canopy.
Machetes—Large heavy knives used for cutting down underbrush.
Mammals—Animals that are warm blooded and have a backbone. The females have glands that produce milk for feeding their young.
Migrate—To move periodically from one region to another for food or breeding.
Mimicry—Having the same shape or color as another organism or objects among which it lives to conceal it and help it to escape predation.
Mutual—A relationship that exists among individuals in which both benefit by the association.
Nocturnal—Occurring or active at night.
Nonrenewable—Not restored or replaced by natural processes.
Nutrients—Substances needed by living things to survive.
Ore—A mineral that is mined to obtain a substance that it contains.
Parasitic—A relationship that exists among individuals in which one benefits and the other is harmed.
Photosynthesis—The process by which green plants make food from water and carbon dioxide in the presence of light.
Plantations—Farms or large estates where a group of plants, often of one kind, is planted, cared for, and sold.
Pollen—The mass of fine grains resembling yellow dust found inside a flower.
Pollination—Transfer of pollen from the male to the female part of the flower.
Predation—The act by which animals hunt, kill, and eat other animals.
Prehensile—Capable of grasping or wrapping around.
Prey—An animal that is hunted by another for food.

Primate—A member of the order of mammals including lemurs, monkeys, apes, and human beings characterized by flexible hands and feet each with five digits.
Reservoir—A natural or artificial lake where water is stored.
Saplings—Young trees.
Species—A category of plants or animals that have common characteristics and are capable of interbreeding.
Spores—Small bodies produced by plants and some lower animals that can grow into new plants or animals.
Stomata—Tiny openings on the outer layer of green leaves.
Stranglers—Plants such as figs that surround a tree, robbing it of its nutrients and causing it to die.
Subsist—To have the minimum that is necessary to exist.
Symbiosis—The living together in close association of two different kinds of organisms.
Synthetic—Produced by chemical means; not found in nature.
Temperate forests—Thick growth of trees and underbrush covering a large area in either of two zones of the earth between the tropics and the polar circles.
Temperate Zone—Either of two zones of the earth between the tropics and the polar circles.
Terrarium—An enclosed container, usually of glass, for keeping small plants or animals indoors.
Timber—Wood used for building things.
Transpiration—The process by which green leaves give off moisture through their stomata.
Tropical Zone—Either of two zones of the earth between the equator and the Temperate Zones.
Understory—The layer of the forest beneath the canopy.

SOURCES OF MORE INFORMATION

Conservation International
1015 18th Street, NW
Suite 1000
Washington, D.C. 20036

Defenders of Wildlife
1244 19th Street, NW
Washington, D.C. 20036

Environmental Defense Fund
1616 P Street, NW
Suite 150
Washington, D.C. 20036

International Union for the Conservation of Nature and Natural Resources
1601 Connecticut Avenue, NW
Washington, D.C. 20009

National Wildlife Federation International Programmes, Resources Conservation Department
1412 16th Street, NW
Washington, D.C. 20036

Nature Conservancy
1800 North Kent Street
Arlington, Virginia 22209

Programme for Belize
P. O. Box 1088
Vineyard Haven, Massachusetts 02568

Public Affairs Office
United States Department of the Interior
Fish and Wildlife Service
Division of Law Enforcement
P. O. Box 3247
Arlington, Virginia 22203

Rainforest Action Network
300 Broadway, Suite 28
San Francisco, California 94133

Smithsonian Tropical Research Institute
900 Jefferson Drive, Suite 2207
Washington, D.C. 20560

Tropical Biology Program
Smithsonian Institution
1000 Jefferson Drive, SW
Washington, D.C. 20560

Wildlife Conservation International
New York Zoological Society
Bronx, New York 10460

World Wildlife Fund
1250 24th Street, NW
Washington, D.C. 20037

SUGGESTED FURTHER READING

Books for Young People

Batten, Mary. *The Tropical Forest: Ants, Ants, Animals & Plants.* New York: Thomas Y. Crowell Company, 1973.

Hecht, Susanna and Alexander Cockburn. *The Fate of the Forest: Developers, Destroyers and Defenders of the Amazon.* London and New York: Verso, 1989.

Jacobs, Una. *Sun Calendar.* Morristown, N.J.: Silver Burdett Press, 1986.

Jennings, Terry. *Tropical Forests.* Freeport, N.Y.: Marshall Cavendish Corporation, 1987.

Kipling, Rudyard. *The Jungle Books.* Garden City, N.Y.: Doubleday and Company, 1948.

Langley, Andrew. *Jungles.* New York: Bookwright Press, 1987.

Leen, Nina. *Monkeys.* New York: Holt, Rinehart, & Winston, 1978.

National Wildlife Federation. *Wonders of the Jungle.* Washington, D.C., 1986.

Nations, James D. *Tropical Rainforests.* New York: Franklin Watts, 1988.

Pope, Joyce. *A Closer Look at Jungles.* New York: Gloucester Press, 1978.

Rowland-Entwistle, Theodore. *Jungles and Rain Forests.* Morristown, N.J.: Silver Burdett Press, 1987.

Other Books

Beddall, Barbara G., ed. *Wallace and Bates in the Tropics.* London: Macmillan, 1969.

Caufield, Catherine. *In the Rainforest.* New York: Alfred A. Knopf, 1985.

Cousteau, Jacques-Yves and Mose Richards. *Jacques Cousteau's Amazon Journey.* New York: Harry N. Abrams, 1984.

Forsyth, Adrian and Ken Miyata. *Tropical Nature.* New York: Charles Scribner's Sons, 1984.

Kaufman, Les and Kenneth Mallory, eds. *The Last Extinction.* Cambridge: MIT Press, 1986.

Kricher, John C. *Neotropical Companion: An Introduction to the Animals, Plants & Ecosystems of the New World Tropics.* Princeton: Princeton University Press, 1989.

Longman, K. A. and J. Jenik. *Tropical Forest and its Environment.* London: Longman, 1974.

Mitchell, Andrew W. *The Enchanted Canopy.* New York: Macmillan, 1986.

Myers, Norman. *The Primary Source.* New York and London: W. W. Norton & Company, 1984.

Perry, Donald. *Life Above the Jungle Floor.* New York: Simon & Schuster, 1986.

Stone, Roger D. *Dreams of Amazonia.* New York: Viking Press, 1985.

Articles

The Ecologist (July–November, 1987), issue on deforestation.

Galvin, Ruth Mehrtens. "Sybaritic to Some, Sinful to Others, but how Sweet It Is." *Smithsonian* (February 1986): 54–64.

Iltis, Hugh H. "Tropical Forests: What Will Be Their Fate?" *Environment* (December 1983): 55–60.

Jackson, Donald Dale. "Making the World a Safer Place for Primates in Peril." *Smithsonian* (December 1985): 100–110.

Jackson, Donald Dale. "Searching for Medicinal Wealth in Amazonia." *Smithsonian* (February 1989): 95–105

Linden, Eugene. "Playing with Fire." *Time* (September 18, 1989): 76–85.

Mittermeier, Russell A. "Monkey in Peril." *National Geographic* (March 1987): 386–395.

Page, Jake. "The 'Island' Arks of Brazil." *Smithsonian* (April 1988): 106–116.

Parfit, Michael. "Whose Hands Will Shape the Future of the Amazon's Green Mansions?" *Smithsonian* (November 1989): 58–74.

"Rain Forests: Tropical Treasures." *Ranger Rick's Nature Scope* (Vol. 4, no. 4, 1989): entire issue.

Raven, Peter. "Tropical Deforestation." *The Science Teacher* (September 1988) 80–87.

Vesilind, Priit J. "Brazil: Moment of Promise & Pain." *National Geographic* (March 1987): 349–385.

White, Peter T. "Rain Forests: Nature's Dwindling Treasures." *National Geographic* (January 1983): 2–46.

Wild, Russell. "Fire at the Equator." *Organic Gardening* (May 1989): 54–59.

INDEX